The author *right* at work, taking
notes, as American collector Norton
Simon, finger raised reprovingly,
protests to the auctioneer during the
sensational sale at Christie's on
March 19, 1965. Immediately before
this photograph was taken
Rembrandt's *Titus* had been knocked
down to Marlborough Fine Art at
740,000 guineas. But, after Mr. Simon
had objected that he was still
bidding, the picture was put up again
and sold to him at 760,000 guineas.
The incident spotlighted an aspect of
saleroom procedure of which the
general public knew nothing – the
business of 'secret bids' and 'bidding
codes'.

ROBERT
WRAIGHT

THE ART GAME AGAIN!

*"Of course, the art scene itself
is probably more disgusting than
it has ever been."*

G. R. Swenson

in *Art and Artists*

LESLIE FREWIN of LONDON

© Robert Wraight, 1965 and 1974

This book, is an updated and extensively rewritten edition of The Art Game, *originally published by Leslie Frewin in 1965. All illustrations, except the Frontispiece and one other photograph, are new to this edition.*

This edition first published 1974 by

Leslie Frewin Publishers Limited,
Five Goodwin's Court,
Saint Martin's Lane,
London WC2N 4LL, England.

This book is set in Garamond Bold Photoset, printed and bound in Great Britain by Weatherby Woolnough, Sanders Road, Wellingborough, Northamptonshire.

ISBN 0 85632 078 1

For

EMMANUEL-CHARLES
BÉNÉZIT

My oldest
and newest
friend

'Art is well known as a game in which one pays for the right to hang on his walls someone else's mental troubles embodied in paint. A game which more often than not leads to expense and fascinates its small circle of devotees who are all convinced that the world needs it, whilst those outside the circle are equally convinced that it does not. As a game art makes sense as long as the entire circle joins in. It stops doing so, at the same time revealing its true nature, as soon as somebody violates the rules, e.g., when Marcel Duchamp submitted a urinal bearing the signature R. Mutt for an exhibition. If the artist is to have his soul's dirty linen pubicly cherished then why not his urinal? Or, for that matter, the contents of his urinal, as Piero Manzoni pointed out.'

– C. BLOK

(of The Gemeente Museum, The Hague)
In *ICA Bulletin* 138/9

List of Illustrations

American millionaire Norton Simon (and
the author) at the sensational Christie's
sale of Rembrandt's *Titus*   *Frontispiece*

Illustration section page

CONTENTS

Preface

Before some book reviewer says it first I must warn the reader that *The Art Game Again!* is not strictly a new book nor is it, strictly, a new edition of *The Art Game.* Indeed it is, as another book reviewer is bound to remark, a bit of a bastard. The first reason for this is that the art trade has undergone such traumatic changes in the ten years since I wrote *The Art Game* that only a completely new book could replace it. The second is that *I* have changed so much that I know I am not the man to write it. The original book was intended as a bit of fun about a subject that fascinated and amused me. And when, shortly after its publication here and in America, I learned from readers' letters that many people were taking it seriously, well, that was flattering, and still fun. But now, when I reflect that the book may have played some part, however small, in attracting to the art game the hordes of Philistines who have changed its nature from bottom to top, I feel like the man who, up before a judge for murdering his mother-in-law, pleaded, 'Honest, m'Lord, I only meant it as a joke.'

Feeling like that, it was inevitable that when I attempted a sequel to *The Art Game* I could not recapture the first careless rapture and wonder with which I had surveyed the inchoate boom of the early sixties. Soon I found that I was writing an anti-art-game book, an exposé of a business in which, as the stakes grew higher and higher, the ethics sank lower and lower. It was to have been called *The Art Rot* and it would, of course, have been unpublishable. Nevertheless, parts of it were salvaged and have been grafted on to, or transplanted into, the

11

present book. I hope that the stitches do not show but I am afraid that the transplants themselves will be made obvious by the air of disillusionment that still clings to them.

For me the art game lost most of its glamour a few years back when bankers and investment companies suddenly found art fascinating, when big business (as distinct from big art-business) moved in, in force, on the art trade and eradicated the last vestiges of the polite pretence that art-dealing had some connexion with Art. I suppose the trend really began when the dealers, Frost and Reed, went public in 1965, but I must admit that, never having had any taste for the sort of pictures that very successful firm deals in, I was unaware of that portentous event until May 1969 when the *Daily Telegraph* cited F. & R.'s chairman as 'the highest paid art dealer in Britain' – with a salary of £44,800 (plus a pension contribution of £12,700) per year.

It was not until the bankers, Rothschilds (who where later to buy the prestigious and once venerated firm of Colnaghi), acquired a bit of Sotheby's in 1970 that it became obvious to me that the rot had set in. About that time, too, I first heard the name *Artemis* tripping off the tongues of the big auctioneers – *Artemis,* is an art investment company backed by Belgium's Banque Lambert. Then, in 1972, the bankers Samuel Montagu bought fifty-one per cent of dealer Richard Green's business, and we learned from *The Times* that David Montagu, the bank's chairman, planned

> to put together a collection of fine art businesses, with a broad spectrum of specializations (including, for example, furniture, silver, and painting dealing specialists) which will one day be floated (hopefully) as a fully-fledged public company it its own right.

12

He is aiming right at the top end of the quality range of art businesses, the idea being that what most art dealers make up for in judgment they tend to lack in finance – which is where the helping hand of Montagu's could be useful.*

If it were not so frightening I might laugh at that phrase – 'where the helping hand of Montagu's could be useful'. The true effect upon the art trade of the helping hands of art-loving bankers and financiers did not take long to emerge and was duly noted by *The Times:*

The availability of large financial backing, and the pressure to trade actively – big brother is watching – is leading to greater competition between dealers. Many observers fear that this is causing an artificial price spiral. (The spiral is a fact, whether artificial or not).

The increasing direct links between the art and antiques market and high finance could make this happy collectors' world as sensitive to economic winds of change as the stock market. Those who fear this is happening point to the investment boom followed by collapse in the silver market between 1967 and 1971. The present boom is going a bit too far too fast for comfort.†

Personally I do not care a damn if investors in art, especially big-business investors, get their fingers burned. It is only in that way that the art trade can return to sanity and that the genuine collector of limited means (for whom *The Art Game* was primarily intended) will be able to survive. And it is only if he is going to survive that there can be any point in having *The Art Game Again!*

1974   R. W.

*The Times, 24 October 1972.
†The Times, 9 February 1973.

Introduction

(to *The Art Game*, 1965)

Artwise, as an American millionaire collector said to me, we live in a remarkable age. An age in which £800,000 is a bargain price for a 'battered, browned, overworked and fuzzed cartoon' (the words are Mr Gerald Reitlinger's, not mine) and a washbasin is exhibited as a work of art (or anti-art?) at the Tate Gallery. An age in which a stapling-machine manufacturer's wife pays £63,000 for a commode to make her husband's life more exciting when he gets home from the factory and a leading artist of the 'Happenings Movement' fills a Paris gallery from floor to ceiling with cartloads of the city's refuse.

Never before has there been so great an interest in art. Never before has the interest on art investments been so great. Never before has art been considered so important a part of education. Never before has education been considered so unimportant a part of art. Never have there been so many artists and art students. Never have there been so many bad artists and art students. Never have so many good and bad books on art poured from the presses or so many reproductions of good and bad pictures been stuck on walls. Never has art been such big business and never has big business attracted so many speculators who want to get in on the act. In fact the art game has become a vast confidence trick for which there is an ever-lengthening queue of willing victims begging to be fleeced. It is said not only that man cannot live by bread alone, but that he cannot live without art. But it is pure cant to pretend that he needs the precious-object-in-the-gilt-frame sort of art that is the prize in the art game. A painting has no instrinsic value. It is a luxury commodity for which a market is deliberately created and maintained by financially interested parties who are neither more nor less noble than the operators of any other legal sort of market. The market value of art is as artificial as that of gold or of diamonds. The great public galleries are the Fort Knoxes of art. Their contents, unseen by the vast majority of the world's population, control the price of art outside them just as surely as the value of money is governed by those obscene, illogical, and ludicrous hoards of gold. In a Utopian world all the Fort Knoxes, of gold or of art, would be abolished. The gold would be used only for filling teeth or making ornaments. The pictures would be given away, one to every person or family. One really good painting in a man's home will do more for him (and maybe for art) than thousands hidden away in the great public mausoleums and in the basements of dealers' galleries.

In my heart I applaud the sentiments of the British artist, Jack Smith, who, when it was suggested that he had come from Sheffield to London because it is easier to sell paintings in the capital, replied: 'That's true. But, oh! This business of selling paintings, and all the ridiculous false values that are placed on works of art. I would like all paintings to be free. I would like the artist to be given an annual salary so that his paintings could be given away to anybody who wanted them. Why not? A good painting is priceless and nobody can afford it really. But also, in the monetary sense of the word, it is valueless. Therefore I would like to take the money element out of art so that perhaps painting would be viewed in rather different terms.'*

In spite of this I am, as is Mr Smith, a player (one of the

*Conversations with Painters, by Noël Barber.

'etceteras' – see *The Art Game, Critics Etcetera)* in the art game and it is therefore to my material benefit to see that the game goes on being played, at least for the rest of my lifetime. Hence the reason for this book, which is intended to attract recruits to the game and to help those recruits to decide which rat-hole (I meant to write 'art' there but my typewriter, which refuses to mince words, wrote 'rat') to choose. It is not another book about the aesthetics or the history of art. It is largely a book about the many and various ways in which money is made out of art and, it follows, the many and various ways of losing money in art. It is not for the highminded but for those who think that art, like sex, should not be taken too seriously. A contemptible book? Perhaps. But before you put it back on the shelf just answer this questionnaire:

1. When the Royal Academy offered the Nation Leonardo da Vinci's cartoon *The Virgin, St Anne and the Infant Christ with St John* for £800,000, did you:

    (a) Send a donation *anonymously* to the Appeal Fund
Or (b) Say, 'What a waste of the taxpayers' money.'
Or (c) Think, 'If it were mine I would have sold it in America
       for twice as much'?

2. When you see the latest thing in *avant-garde* art do you say:

    (a) It can't be just a legpull.
Or (b) It's just a legpull.
Or (c) I could pull legs like that?

3. When you read about a forger who has fooled the art experts do you say:

(a) How terrible.
Or (b) How funny.
Or (c) How clever?

4. If a 'knocker' (see Chapter Five of *The Art Game,* 'Forgeries, Fakes and Fiddles') came to your home and offered a hundred pounds for that worthless little picture grandmother left you, would you:

(a) Tell him it is not for sale at any price.
Or (b) Take his money.
Or (c) Put him off until you can get an expert valuation of it?

If your answers to all four questions are (a) then by all means put the book down at once and keep your illusions. If all of your answers are (b) it is not for you either. You are not such stuff as the art game is played on. But if all, or any, of your answers are (c) the book is yours. Work hard at it and you can join the game. However low (or high) you may be there is a place for you, if you really try, among the collectors, the investors, the dealers, the runners, the knockers, the auctioneers, the experts, the critics, the art historians, the museum wallahs, the art gossipmongers, the forgers, the publicists, the phoney art-teachers, the culture-hawkers, the vendors of artists' materials and of painting holidays, the pseudo-Impressionists, the 'pupils of Annigoni', the rubbish collagists, the neo-primitives and, last and least likely, the PBGA.*

*The poor bloody genuine artists.

Don't lose any time because, as artist-critic Ad Reinhardt 'the black monk' of the New York School, prophesies, *The next revolution in Art will see the disappearance of personal art-dealing, private art-collecting and individual artist-enterprising, of personalistic, privateering art – 'pricing, buying and selling'.*

Now read on.

R. W. 1965

1

Royal Magpies and Common Marmots

To collect nothing at all is to descend below the level of magpies and marmots.

GERALD REITLINGER

Without covetousness you are not going to have an appreciation of art. And I think that if covetousness by some magic was destroyed art would come to an end. It's very rare to be able to appreciate art without wanting to own it.

PETER WILSON, Chairman of Sotheby's, in an
interview on the BBC Third Programme

A collector is someone interested in art for his own self-ennoblement. Nowadays people buy paintings mostly out of snobbery or to avoid tax.

PEGGY GUGGENHEIM

The art game is very old. The Greeks played it and the Romans played it. In more modern civilisations it was first played only by kings and great noblemen. Henry VIII played a rudimentary form of it but Charles I, who acquired a taste for collecting from his older brother, Henry, Prince of Wales, was the first royal 'division one' player in this country. He is said to have had a 'good nose' for pictures (there were two Rembrandts in his collection while the artist was still young and little known) and he employed a team of agents to scour Europe, and particularly Italy, for new acquisitions. Usually the activities of these agents were shrouded in a cloak-and-dagger air of mystery for fear of such rival collectors as Cardinal Richelieu and the Grand Duke of Tuscany. He encouraged his courtiers to make him gifts of paintings and his ambassadors to bring paintings back to him from their trips abroad. Sometimes he would make exchanges with other collectors, a Leonardo for a Holbein and a Titian, a volume of Holbein portraits for Raphael's *St George*. By his virtuoso gamesmanship he amassed, in the space of twenty years, an almost incomparable collection.

Then along came Cromwell, and after the King's execution in 1649 the collection was confiscated by the Commonwealth. An inventory was made in which each picture was valued and then the dispersal of the collection was begun. First a number of works were reserved by Cromwell for official purposes. Among them were the great Raphael Cartoons (now in the Victoria and Albert Museum) which were valued at £300. A second group of pictures was allotted to be used to pay various creditors of the Court, and a third group was offered for sale.

Many of the pictures in the second group were never collected but remained in the palaces until the Restoration when, with these unclaimed works as a nucleus, Charles II began his efforts to re-build his father's collection.

The job was an impossible one. Most of the greatest treasures in the third group had been bought by dealers and sold to such European collectors as the King of Spain, the Archduke Leopold William of Austria, and Cardinal Mazarin. Among them were Giorgione's *Concert Champêtre* and a superb collection of Titians, all now in the Louvre, Raphael's *La Perla,* now in the Prado, and many of today's most prized masterpieces in the great museums of other European countries. But if these things were out of Charles's reach others, bought by English collectors, were not. A Royal Commission, whose methods were, to put it mildly, unethical, was set up to direct the recovery.

Acting upon reports supplied by special informers, the Commission brought certain pressures to bear which provoked such a flow of 'gifts' to the King that numerically, at least, a major part of the Royal Collection was reconstituted.

To paraphrase the comment of the art historian, Wilhelm von Bode, on the American banker, Pierpont Morgan, Charles II was the first Englishman who was determined to possess everything of the best, if it were not already in private hands. Indeed, even if it *were* already in private hands; for, although the rules of the art game have become more complicated and the number of players has vastly increased, the principal goal was then, as now, to provide people who already had all the necessities of life with an overt way of showing who were the top dogs. Keeping up with the Joneses artwise was, in the 17th century, a matter of keeping up with the Stuarts. Then, as now, it thrived on covetousness and snobbery. Only the quality of the snobbery has changed. The change, from a predominantly intellectual snobbery to a predominantly 'money' snobbery, came about, according to Ernst Fischer, with the growth of capitalism:

For the capitalist luxury may mean the purely private satisfaction of his desires, but it also means the chance of displaying his wealth for prestige reasons. Capitalism is not essentially a social force that is well disposed to art or that promotes art; in so far as the average capitalist needs art at all, he needs it as an embellishment of his private life or else as a good investment.*

Such a capitalist collector was the Russian-born John Julius Angerstein, the 'father of the modern Lloyd's', whose pictures, bought by Parliament after his death in 1823, formed the foundation of the National Gallery. Of him Sir Philip Hendy, Director of the National Gallery from 1946 to 1967, has written:

It has been said that he was a new type of collector in that his acquisition of pictures was also an acquisition of prestige. His was certainly not the first collection which was intended to bring prestige to its owner; but as a self-made man of foreign birth 'considered deficient in Education' he may well have relied on his pictures to express something that he did not know how to express himself. They were certainly the chief instrument of the peculiar position which he made for himself 'at the West End of the town'. Several of the leading artists and collectors were often to be found at 100 Pall Mall, where he kept open house and hospitable board and built a gallery for his collection. As the collection increased, more and more visitors were allowed to see it, until not to have seen Mr. Angerstein's pictures was to be socially unfinished.†

One hundred years after Angerstein, the astonishing Joseph Duveen was to exploit, on a vast scale, the capitalist's demand

*The Necessity of Art, a Marxist Approach, by Ernst Fischer.
†The National Gallery, London, by Philip Hendy.

for prestige-giving art which by then had flowered mightily in America. Duveen's enormous success as a dealer lay in the fact that he understood better than any dealer before him the nature of the hunger for prestige felt by the great capitalist emperors. He knew because he had the hunger himself. He was no great art expert, he had no need to be, he could afford to hire any expert he liked, but as a practical psychologist he was, and still is, without equal in the art game. He knew, in the first place, that if you are selling prestige it is no good offering it cheap. In a society in which prestige is based on money the more you pay the more you get. It followed, too, that the more *he* paid the more prestige *he* got. For this reason he delighted in publicity. Not for him the secret deal. Whether he was buying or selling he let the facts be known as widely as possible. 'When you pay high for the priceless, you're getting it cheap,' he told his millionaire clients and then conditioned them to the privilege, as one of them put it, of paying a premium for the privilege of paying the highest price for the priceless.

In his book on Duveen,* S N Behrman tells anecdote after anecdote illustrating the almost childlike faith that these great tycoons had in Duveen. There was H E Huntington, confessing to a member of Duveen's staff that if Duveen told him a pair of ordinary andirons were remarkable and worth $75,000 he would gladly pay up. There was Jules Bache, gratefully agreeing to guarantee Duveen a one hundred per cent profit on anything the dealer deigned to offer him. There was Henry Clay Frick, overcome by Duveen's generosity in letting him have a Gainsborough for $300,000 and overlooking the fact that if Duveen had not deliberately outbid Knoedler's, who, he knew were acting for Frick, he would have got it much cheaper. And

*Duveen, by S N Behrman

25

there was the great Andrew Mellon, thanking Duveen for letting him buy the contents of his apartment – for twenty-one million dollars. To all of these, and dozens of other millionaire collectors whose thirst for prestige-art he set out to slake at prices even higher than those of today, Duveen presented himself as a St Peter through whose grace alone they could get passes, albeit very expensive ones, to immortality. He seemed able to turn every general adversity to his personal advantage. When taxation and death duties threatened to end the millionaires' picture-buying bonanza he showed his clients that:

> The public bequest, impervious to taxation was the way out. Specifically, the public bequest of Duveens was the way out. By ear-marking his purchases for museums, a collector could afford to buy art; at least he could let art pass through his hands on the way to the museums from Duveen. Gifts to museums offered his clients not merely economy but immortality. Using Duveen's method an aged American millionaire could, in good conscience, circumvent oblivion and the Collector of Internal Revenue at a single stroke. Under Duveen's spell, one after another of his clients – H E Huntington, Frick, Mellon, Bache, Kress – took up this form of philanthropy. For Duveen the advantage was double; with museums as the terminal for his pictures, he no longer had to worry about the passing of the big houses – the museums were larger than the houses – and he no longer had to worry that the pictures would be dumped back on the market at a time when it might be difficult for him to sell them, especially at the prices he would have to charge after buying back at Duveen prices.*

The 'public bequest' system, the American system whereby a private citizen who buys works of art gets a substantial tax concession if he undertakes to leave those works of art to a

*Duveen, by S N Behrman

26

museum when he dies, has had a very far-reaching effect on the art game. In the first place it meant that American collectors had a financial advantage over other collectors. They were given what amounted to a Government subsidy which, like any subsidy given to purchasers rather than sellers, led to an increase in prices. But it did much more than that. It made the art market attractive to a new type of collector, one who cared nothing about art and was interested initially not even in its prestige-giving properties, but in its tax-exemption (and, needless to say, its tax-evasion) possibilities. Having joined in the art game such a 'collector' would then, of course, discover that it offered much more than tax exemption and begin to learn to enjoy those others of art's present built-in boons – prestige and profit. By comparison with the new-style American collector who has come to art in this way such men as Mellon and Morgan and Huntington were art-for-art's sake aesthetes. This sort of collector, more than any before him, has equated the possession of works of art with the possession of money and his example has inevitably been followed in countries where no tax-dodging inducement is offered. He is a gift to those dealers who, now that the best Old Masters and Impressionist pictures are nearly all locked up in museums, are promoting modern art and artists by every means known to high-pressure sales-manship.

There are still, of course, some collectors of integrity and great knowledge, even in America, but these people are not a part of the art game as it is played today. They cannot be led by the nose or made the fools of dealer-inspired fashion but follow their own taste and conviction and get a satisfaction and pleasure that has nothing to do with the envy of others. Indeed they are often collecting the works of artists who are unpopular

27

and probably unknown to the type of collector who predominates today, the new-rich tycoon who has devoted his whole life to making money only to discover that he has nothing except the things that money can buy. One of these things, however, is the outward appearance of culture. And this means paintings. Almost invariably, when I have talked to any collector of this sort in Britain he has claimed at some point that he was 'always interested in art as a boy'. But this does not mean that he now buys the paintings he likes (in this respect his Victorian forerunner, who paid £10,000 for a bad Landseer and 7,000 guineas for an Albert Moore in preference to an Italian Primitive, was more praiseworthy). He has probably had no time to develop even bad taste of his own and must now rely entirely on the knowledge of an expert who can tell him that such and such pictures are the ones he ought to have and can give him the assurances he wants that they are good investments. What can happen to this tycoon-type collector when he tries to 'go it alone' is amusingly illustrated by the story of a holiday-camp king who, after negotiating to buy the late William de Belleroche's huge collection of pictures by Brangwyn for £20,000, suddenly lost interest. He gave no reason but, the vendor told me, until the last minute he thought he was going to get several hundred Gauguins for his £20,000.

In America the collector who invests in pictures and the prestige that goes with them is generally franker than his British counterpart. 'My passion is for the Impressionists, and dollarwise they are also great,' said one Texas collector quoted by John Bainbridge in *The Super-Americans*. Another, when told by a friend that his collection of Picassos made him a Communist in the eyes of 'local patriots', replied, 'You can tell those sons of bitches over there that I've made a quarter of a million dollars on these paintings so far. That will shut them up, because that's the kind of language they understand'.* It is, of course the language most of us understand. It is the language of the art game. It has succeeded, where Esperanto has failed, in becoming a universal language. Whereas in the past it was spoken only in whispers by consenting art dealers in private, today it is shouted, by property magnates and oil men, grocery tycoons, and shipowners, stockbrokers, and washing-machine manufacturers from Bond Street to Madison Avenue, from Venice to Tokyo, from Paris to São Paulo. The whole business of collecting is now so vulgarised that ultimately it must defeat its own end, and instead of being a symbol of culture a collection of what the auctioneers call 'Impressionist and Modern' works of art will signify philistinism and the crudest sort of materialism.

In the 1960s we saw the greatest of international art shows, the Venice Biennale, turned into a Babel-onian market at which dealers, gallery proprietors, critics, collectors, and artists behave just like any other businessmen at an international trade show. The booze flows continuously for days, the expense accounts and the old pals' acts are worked overtime, deals are fixed, bribes are paid, reputations are invented, publicity stunts are thought up. But it would be wrong to think that in all this the 'collector' is the poor gullible victim of rapacious dealers. He is, rather, their collaborator. He likes to pay high prices. He likes to pay high prices not for the thrill of being extravagant or for the publicity it may bring him (although both these are important to him) but because by supporting the dealer's efforts to upgrade the prices of a particular artist he is improving his own investment in that artist. There is a whole class of collec-

*The Super-Americans, by John Bainbridge.

tors today, as any dealer will tell you, which is not interested in getting anything cheap. They are suspicious of it. The reason is simple. The only thing they understand is money, and their admiration for any picture is almost invariably in direct proportion to the amount paid for it. They have no built-in criteria by which to judge a work of art either technically or aesthetically and are obliged to work on the assumption that the most expensive things in the world are the best. This is something we are all obliged to do to some extent when buying things of which we have no special knowledge. We are dependent almost entirely upon the honesty of the retailer who tells us that this watch is worth twice as much as that one or that this wool is far better quality than that and therefore worth paying more for. And because generally the retailer is honest these things are so. If then money is no problem we buy the most expensive of everything because we want the best. We shop in Bond Street instead of Kensington High Street even though we may believe that the difference in quality does not wholly justify the difference in price.

The commonest type of big art collector is a man who has vastly more money than sensibility. If he is a fool he goes around, like certain Texan collectors (they would be more correctly called 'accumulators'), buying in bulk according to his own whims (as the undiscriminating patron of living artists he may, by chance, be doing a service to contemporary art but it is much more likely that by his lack of discrimination he is encouraging the phoney and the worthless). If he is shrewd he puts himself in the hands of a well-established dealer and lets him build up a collection for him, a collection that is primarily a sound investment and only incidentally a group of works of art.

His attitude to art has infected everyone else in the art game: the artists, the dealers, the auctioneers, the public and private patrons, the smaller collectors, even the critics. Largely because of him the art trade has lost the last little bit of that dignity that once raised it above other forms of trade. Now it has become a business like any other for marketing a commodity at the biggest possible rate of profit.

Buying pictures for love of art is virtually a thing of the past. Constantly regaled by the Press with stories about fortunes, large and small, made out of art every day, even the most ingenuous picture buyer finds himself wondering how much his picture will be worth in the future. From there it is only a short step to buying pictures with thoughts of profit uppermost in his mind. And having reached that stage there can be no going back. He cannot regain his innocence, he can only go forward inspired by the knowledge that there is easy money to be made from art by anyone who takes the trouble to learn the ropes (or can buy up the man who knows the ropes).

The feeling that a boom cannot last for ever will give him a sense of urgency. He will soon discover that in order to succeed there must be no more love-of-art stuff in his thinking. 'Art, like business, is business', must be his motto. He will learn to stand outside art and look at it dispassionately, with cold, mean, stockbrokerish eyes and be as objective as a butcher sizing up livestock. He will learn to recognise a new fashion in the early stages of gestation and smell the first whiff of death about a moribund one. He will learn what to buy and when and where to buy it, how much it is worth, how much to pay for it and where and for how much to sell it at any particular time. He will learn not to buy anything simply because he likes it and to buy things he hates if they look like good investments. He will

31

learn the tricks of the trade and how to counter them with knowledge and cunning of his own or of others whose brains he can pick.

What follows is an attempt to reveal to him some of the rules of a game that has no rules. A game which was once the preserve of kings and nobles but is now wide open to the lowest in the land, whether banker or burglar, stockbroker or scrap-merchant, property tycoon or ponce, politician or Pop-star.

2

Art For Money's Sake

The total number of authentic, accepted paintings by Michelangelo can be counted on the fingers and we can dispense with him as part of the art market. His fresco painting in the Sistine Chapel might well be considered the most valuable work of art in the world, but we can be fairly certain that it will never be sold.

RICHARD H RUSH

The extraordinary quotation above (it is almost as good as Duveen's 'If I had the Sistine Chapel, I could sell it tomorrow half-a-dozen times over') is taken from a book, *Art as an Investment,* published in America in 1961. The author, Richard H Rush, is the holder of the degrees of Master of Business Administration and Doctor of Commercial Science awarded by the Harvard Graduate School of Business Administration, and is also an investment banker, an ardent amateur of art and the owner of a collection of pictures valued (in 1961) at 'more than one-half million dollars'. The book, widely reviewed on publication, drew from the *Wall Street Journal* the comment that Mr Rush had 'almost succeeded in applying Dow-Jones averaging techniques to the suddenly expanding world of art

33

brokerage' but had not 'quite managed to come up with a suggestion for an "art exchange" page that would be equivalent to an ordinary stock exchange page, because the 6,000 extant Renoir paintings, for example, can't be averaged for a useful ticker-tape quotation'! Nevertheless, his advice was no less valuable than that of those selfless altruists the City editors, racing tipsters, and football-pools experts who, while telling us how to get rich quick, never seem to take their own advice.

Thoughtfully, Mr Rush did not pitch his advice in highflown terms. He used an easy American style familiar to anyone who watches old Hollywood films on television. Example: 'His paintings of peasant life bring in the low four figures, and his Cubist period works sometimes sell in the low five figures.' He was, pardonably, a bit shaky on British paintings and painters. After all, Gainsborough himself thought that he ought to have been *Sir* Thomas, and if William Holman Hunt (1827-1910) is not (along with Victor Passmore *(sic)*, Stanley Spencer, Philip Wilson Steer, and Alan Reynolds!) exactly 'a leading name of the Contemporary British School', well, he was once. Less easily forgiven was his summing-up of an account of Hitler's persecution of such great artists as Beckmann, Kandinsky, and Klee. 'The ironical part about this policy of Hitler', he wrote, 'was that while Hitler himself painted pictures and several have appeared on the auction market recently, he painted no better than the Expressionists'! And one's faith in his judgement was a little shaken when, after saying that what makes an artist great is his power to add something new to the art of painting, he cited Annigoni, alongside Raphael, as an example of quality, 'The essence of art value'.

Such imperfections apart, however, the book was remarkable

34

in several ways. It was full of hardheaded horse-sense couched in the most forthright terms completely free of that namby-pamby aesthetics stuff. When, for instance, Mr Rush wanted to say, 'Don't put all your art-eggs in one basket', he wrote: 'To own just one painting is like investing all of one's assets in one stock. Standard Oil Company of New Jersey is certainly a fine company and its stock is good, but there is merit to the attitude that it might not rise as surely as would a portfolio of selected stocks. There is the additional disadvantage in owning just one painting as against owning one kind of stock one always knows the value of the one stock, but he doesn't know the value of the one painting until he offers it for sale.' But it was remarkable chiefly because (so far as I am aware) it was the first book to come out openly and treat the art-business as one might treat any other business. By means of price lists and a number of graphs it sought to give an accurate picture of all the major price movements, over the previous thirty or thirty-five years. Of these the *Wall Street Journal* remarked:

> To judge by Mr Rush's graphs, those art investors who have gone in for French post-impressionism and French 'modern' have done considerably better for themselves than investors in most electronics or chemical stocks. Lumping the three post-impressionist leaders, Van Gogh, Gauguin, and Cézanne, together for instance, Mr Rush produces an absolutely dizzy ascending curve. Taking 1930 for his base year of 100, Mr Rush finds the Van Gogh-Gauguin-Cézanne trio hitting 177% in 1950, 566% in 1955, and 4,833% in 1960.

Surprisingly no one who reviewed the book thought to suggest to Mr Rush that he should write a second volume which would tell us, not what had happened to prices in the preceding twenty-five years, but what was going to happen to

35

them in the next twenty-five. In the absence of such a book I essayed, in the 1965 edition of *The Art Game,* to make good this omission in a chapter called 'Tomorrow's Winners'. In it I listed more than two hundred artists whose works I believed would prove to be good investments. That ninety-five per cent of my forecasts have already proved correct is nothing to be proud of. In the past decade virtually everything has gone up and, in spite of the old saying, virtually nothing has come down. If I had listed every one of the thousands of artists named in Bénézit's eight-volume *Dictionnaire,* my success ratio would probably have been the same. That I named so few artists is itself indicative of the fantastic explosion that has taken place in the art trade since 1965, for my list was largely drawn from Christie's and Sotheby's catalogues of the previous decade and, while omitting those masters of all periods whose pictures were already 'out of reach for all but the world's biggest public galleries and private Croesuses', it did embrace most of those other artists whose works were continually offered to the great auction houses and *considered by them to be worthy of inclusion in their sales.*

Now, in the 1970s, the stupendous quantity of 'art' that is changing hands through the agency of auctioneers and dealers is even more phenomenal than the heights to which record prices for individual paintings have soared. So diminished is the 'real' value of the pound that the all-time saleroom record of £2,310,000 paid at Christie's in 1970 for Velasquez's *Juan de Pareja* may really be no record at all. Comparisons with earlier periods become increasingly difficult to make the further we go back, but some of the prices paid in the eighteenth and nine-teenth centuries were no less astonishing to the people of those days than today's gasp-making prices are to us. Indeed, in the

1920s the great American millionaires frequently paid prices comparable with, and perhaps greater than, those of today. The $750,000 that Duveen charged Alfred W Erickson for Rembrandt's *Aristotle* in 1928 was worth much the same as the $2,300,000 the picture fetched at auction in New York in 1961. And it should not, I think, be far out to guess that the purchasing power of a 1961 dollar was very nearly the same as a 1974 pound. Certain it is that the *Aristotle* would fetch two million pounds today. The $600,000 that Henry Huntington paid Duveen in 1921 for Gainsborough's *Blue Boy* was worth something like five times as much as the £130,000 Agnews gave in 1960 for the same artist's *Mr and Mrs Andrews in a Park* (now in the National Gallery, London) and three to four times as much as the £280,000 paid at Sothebys in 1972 for his *The Gravenor Family**. The $1,166,000 paid by Andrew Mellon in 1931, the middle of the Great Depression, for Raphael's *Alba Madonna* was equivalent to at least two million of those paltry pounds in your pocket (but do not imagine you could buy such a picture for a mere two million today – five million would be nearer the mark).

It is, of course, idle to speculate upon the prices that masterpieces already in the great museums might fetch if they were for sale. Idle but fascinating, as was the case when, in 1965, an official valuation was made of 600 paintings in the Uffizi Gallery, Florence. The total, £214 million, included £14 million for Botticelli's *Primavera* and £10$\frac{3}{4}$ million for his *Birth of Venus*. Leonardo's *Annunciation* and *Adoration of the Magi* were valued at £9 million and £3$\frac{1}{2}$ million respectively, both of which seemed modest, when compared with the £40 million for which the *Mona Lisa* was reported to have been valued for

*See page 152

insurance in 1962, and very realistic, when compared with the £2 million paid by the National Gallery, Washington, in 1967 for the same artist's little (42 by 37 cm.) portrait of *Ginevra dei Benci*. The effect of scarcity upon prices is, then, always incalculable – and often ridiculous as was seen in 1962 when, following the purchase for our National Gallery of Leonardo's cartoon, *The Virgin, St Anne and the Infant Christ with St John*, for £800,000, it was made known that several American museums had been ready to pay £$1\frac{1}{2}$ million and at least one would have gone up to £2 million.

In a sense every painting has a scarcity value because it is unique, but this scarcity value cannot be translated into terms of money until more than one person wants it (or covets it, as Peter Wilson has put it), and is prepared to pay for it. To these people the picture is to some degree a rarity in the sense that it is the one they want, at a particular time, in preference to all others. A struggle between two such potential buyers who happen to have large financial resources is usually behind the freak price that hits the headlines. Thus, two bidders (today they could be investment trusts or banks) whose reasons for wanting a particular painting may have very little to do with art, may yet start a new demand for a particular artist's work at hitherto undreamed-of prices.

Several examples of this come immediately to mind. One was in 1957 when the Greek shipowner Stavros Niarchos, bidding, so it is said, against another Greek shipowner who is related to him, paid £104,630 in a Paris saleroom for a still life of apples by Gauguin. Both men were later rumoured to have been anxious to dispose of large quantities of French francs before a threatened devaluation of the currency took place. The previous saleroom record for a Gauguin was, I believe, £17,000 paid a month earlier at Sothebys for a rather dull work of the artist's Brittany period. Yet before the year was out the artist's Tahitian picture *Mao Taporo* realised £64,330 in New York. And in 1959 *J'attends ta réponse* made £130,000 at Sotheby's.

Another example was the remarkable case of *La Belle Strasbourgeoise,* by Nicolas de Largillière, bought by the City of Strasbourg at Sotheby's in July 1963 for £145,000. The underbidder was a New York dealer presumably acting on behalf of a client. A year or two before the Second World War the same picture had fetched almost exactly one-tenth as much and was for some time the highest auction-priced French picture on record. Here, it seemed clear, was an outstanding instance of the subject matter of a painting being of paramount importance. It is certainly an exquisite example of early eighteenth-century French portraiture but, had the woman in the picture been wearing fashionable Parisian clothes of the period instead of the regional costume of Strasbourg, it would probably not have fetched more than fifty thousand pounds in 1963. Indeed Sotheby's anticipated a price of about £45,000.

As is usual after such a surprise boost in price for a minor master the salerooms were suddenly inundated with 'Largillières'. Most of them were not by Largillière at all, a few were hack works of the sort that even the best portrait-painter turns out when he is more interested in his fee than in his sitter. It was not until June 1964, when Christie's were entrusted with the sale of a group of portraits of the Throckmorton family, that the effect of the freak price for *La Belle Strasbourgeoise* could be seen. Estimates by the pundits of Bond Street (and, apparently, those of Christie's, too) put a top price of £35,000 on a flamboyant portrait of Sir Robert Throckmorton and considerably lower figures on the portraits of his daughter

Elizabeth and his aunt Anne, both of whom were painted in nun's habit. The first picture to come up was that of Elizabeth Throckmorton. After a duel which had even the imperturbable Geoffrey Agnew, the most experienced of saleroom duellists, visibly clenching perspiring hands, it was knocked down to Agnew's for 62,000 guineas (Christie's still adhere to this non-existent coinage which irritates the buyer but brings in a few – or, as in this case, many thousand – extra shillings).* The portrait of Sir Robert was knocked down at 55,000 guineas and the portrait of Aunt Anne at 38,000 guineas. Largillière, who does not rate a single mention in Gerald Reitlinger's compendious history of art prices, *The Economics of Taste,* was confirmed as one of the fashionable and high-priced artists of our time.

Also in 1964 there was an interesting sequel to the case of *La Belle Strasbourgeoise,* when a second version of the picture, comparable in quality with the first, turned up in the showrooms of Frank Partridge & Sons, exactly opposite Sotheby's in New Bond Street. It had been in the family of Major Edward Baring of Rye, Sussex, for seventy years, was now offered for sale at only £70,000. There were no immediate takers. What had happened to the underbidder for the £145,000 picture? Why didn't he jump at the opportunity of getting an equally fine picture of the same subject by the same artist at less than half the price? Did the fact that *La Belle* was now no longer unique but had a twin make all that difference?

*When Britain's coinage was decimalised in 1971 it was generally expected that this nonsense would end. But Christie's blandly redefined the 21-shilling guinea as £1.05 and carried on as before. There is no doubt that this anachronistic system works in favour of the seller and against the buyer. For, in the heat of the sale, the buyer invariably thinks in nice round numbers of pounds and forgets all those odd pence which will go a long way towards paying the commission that Christie's charge the seller.

We may be fairly certain that, had the existence of the second picture been known at the time the first one was sold at Sothebys, neither version would have been valued at anything like £145,000.

Of course, hundreds of sudden price-jumps on a lower lever, heralding a new fashion for this or that minor artist have been witnessed in recent years. I have particular reasons for remembering several of them. When, for example, the prices of drawings that poor Walter Greaves had been glad to sell for 'five bob' at the end of his life, abruptly rose in the salerooms from £10 or £15 to £100 and more, I had just sold a collection for a few pounds profit. Apparently I was the only dealer who did not know that a new book about Greaves, *Chelsea Reach* by Tom Pocock, was about to be published and that it would spark off a spate of Greaves exhibitions. Then there was the time – the first and last time – I answered one of those advertisements in the quality newspapers. 'Private Collector wishes to purchase a painting by Atkinson Grimshaw', it said. When the 'private collector' saw my Grimshaw, tears came into his eyes. The price of the picture was £650 but he could not possibly scrape together more than £500. He had even brought his father-in-law along to confirm this sad fact. Embarrassed by the sight of a grown man standing in the middle of my little gallery with tears in his eyes, and touched by the whines of father-in-law, who obviously cared so much for son-in-law's happiness, I gave in. The younger man reached for his cheque book and was about to write his cheque when the older man pulled from his own pocket a thick roll of fivers and asked me, 'Will you take £475 in cash instead?' I would not. Then we, the young man and I, carried the picture – it was a big one – out of the gallery and around the corner to where a shiny new Jaguar was waiting to receive it. As it was a Sunday they cannot have driven straight to Christie's but they must have gone there as soon as possible; for, two or three months later, it was all in the *Daily Telegraph*. 'Record 1,900 guineas for Grimshaw' read the headline. John Atkinson Grimshaw was confirmed as a very good investment and prices for his work, which had been moving up steadily along with those of many other Victorian artists, leapt up overnight more than a hundred per cent.

Towards the end of 1973 a very large watercolour by that rather mediocre and rather naïve marine artist, Samuel Owen (c 1768-1857), was sold at the Phillips saleroom in London for £2,200, about six times as much as the previous record price. Having seen the picture only across the saleroom I assumed that it must have been an outstanding work, the artist's masterpiece (if a mediocre artist can have a masterpiece) and that the price was a flash-in-the-pan that was unlikely to be repeated. But for their sale two weeks later Phillips rustled up two small, run-of-the-mill 'Sam' Owens, that not even the artist's mother could have called 'masterpieces', and sold them for £1400 and £800.

Since, as we have seen, a single phenomenal price may raise the general price of an artist's entire output, it could be to a dealer's advantage to arrange to buy at an exceptionally high price a single picture by an artist of whose pictures he has a stock. The buying must be done publicly, ie at auction, where it may be reported in the Press or, at least, will be seen by a large section of the picture-dealing and picture-buying public. The picture will have been put into the sale by the dealer, probably under another name, and he then bids for it against an accomplice until the right price has been reached. The cost to the dealer will be ten per cent (the trade rate charged by the big London auctioneers for items between £500 and £10,000) of the knock-down price of the picture. If now, instead of throwing his whole stock of the artist's work on to the market, he lets it dribble out slowly, thus creating the impression of scarcity the gamble may pay off handsomely.

It would take a Joe Duveen to do this in the grand manner but on a small scale it has frequently been done to boost the prices of certain Victorian artists and some of the minor Impressionists. It has also been used by some dealers to justify the raising of prices for the work of living artists for whom they act as agents. It can be regarded, I suppose, as just another method of publicising a product, no more reprehensible than any other method and more effective than most.

Publicity of a more orthodox kind has played an increasingly important part in recent years in the art market. In a radio interview Peter Wilson, of Sotheby's, said that he did not think that publicity could do anything for an artist's work unless the artist had 'got something'. From the auctioneer's viewpoint this is probably true, for the saleroom can be a graveyard for the phoney. Many a sham artist in the fifties and sixties made quick and easy money out of exhibitions based on publicity gimmicks and little more, but when his pictures reached the saleroom their owners had a shock. Sothebys have themselves made use of publicity to great advantage during the past fifteen years. In an article called 'Values behind the value' the art critic of the *Daily Telegraph,* Terence Mullaly, wrote that a 'potent influence upon prices is exerted by carefully controlled publicity, by the establishment of an aura of prestige around a particular auction room', an obvious allusion to Sotheby's. But the 'aura of prestige' surrounding Sotheby's began with the Goldschmidt Sale of 1958 – before the firm began to employ publicity men. It was primarily a product of the enterprising way in which Sotheby's took advantage of the removal in 1954 of restrictions on imports from the United States. After the largely unsolicited publicity brought by that sale interest in art prices (not to be confused with interest in art) suddenly blossomed profusely. It became fashionable to be able to talk about the latest spectacular sale as if it were the latest first night. In the 1760s, Sir Alec Martin tells us, young ladies were warned by fashionable writers that a visit to Christie's was the correct thing to do during the London season. In the 1960s it was Sotheby's turn.

As a result of all the publicity the number of people playing the art game increased enormously. Before the sixties were out there was virtually nothing left – after the predations of the museums, the big dealers, and the wealthier collector-investors – to circulate among the small-time dealers and the hordes of *marchands-amateurs*. Such people could hardly hope to get their hands on even the sweepings of the fashionable artists' studios, so the problems of supplying the needs of hundreds of thousands of new collectors looked formidable. But in the event there was no problem. For at the lower end of the trade it was soon realised that it was no longer necessary to find artists, dead or alive, whose work could be made fashionable enough for the new collectors to collect. 'Collecting' itself had become the fashion. Reitlinger was proved right. Everyone, it seemed, had decided that 'to collect nothing at all is to descend below the level of magpies and marmots'. And for them nothing, however trivial, however worthless (even in terms of money), however despicable, was to be excluded from their lunatic acquisitiveness. So the climate was made right for the cheat and the fraud and the smart-operator to flourish.

3

Fashionable
Nonentities, Etc

*Prosperity crowns those who ride the waves of fashion with a
timing nice enough to slip from one to another before each breaks.*
JOHN I H BAUR, Associate Director,
Whitney Museum of American Art

*Fahion is a sorcerer's charm or talisman changing the masterpiece
of today into the laughing stock of tomorrow.*
MAURICE RHEIMS *Art on the Market, 1961*

In the preface to this book I noted how the injection into the
art trade of large amounts of investment capital had brought
about spectacular new record prices for pictures since 1970.
The most remarkable of such prices were not the huge ones
paid for the few important works by great masters whose names
are familiar to the general public; they were to be expected.
Even the staggering £609,000 paid at Christies in June 1973 for
a landscape by Aelbert Cuyp, whose name is scarcely a
household word, was not for me the most remarkable, for that

was a masterpiece by an important and influential master. What I found most extraordinary – and distressing – were the absurdly inflated prices that were paid for the works of artists who were, until a few years ago, quite rightly considered to be nonentities.

Scarcity coupled with inflation was bound to bring phenomenal prices for important pictures and such prices were bound to be reflected to some extent in the prices of lesser works. But this cannot explain the crazy prices – sometimes tens of thousands of pounds – that are now being paid for pictures that were churned out by prolific mediocrities in the nineteenth century and bought by our great-grandfathers on both sides of the Channel to break up the all-over patterns of the wallpaper. The main reason for this madness is, I believe, that the old discerning picture-collecting public, who used to be the ultimate arbiters of price, have been ousted by a new picture-acquiring-for-moneymaking public who are completely lacking in discernment and who, at art auctions, appear to operate on the assumption that the more they pay for a picture the better it must be.

In the old days of the 1950s and 1960s this would have been fatal, but today there are so many people who think this way that, in their freak world, there seems to be no problems in 'turning over' any picture so long as the price is high enough. I am quite convinced, from my own observations, that many a fashion for a particular artist's work has started as a result of two members of this idiot brigade bidding against each other in the saleroom. Each thinks the other knows more than he does, which is not difficult because neither knows anything. So the picture, which is worth, say £500, is knocked down for £2,000. Then as soon as the sale is over another member of the brigade approaches the 'successful' bidder and offers him a 'quick profit' of £500. After a few weeks the picture will probably have changed hands two or three times and ended up in a small but smart West End gallery, priced at £5,000. In the meantime everyone whose hands the picture has passed through, and dozens of other people as well, are on the lookout for more pictures by the same artist. So when a second does turn up in a sale, it fetches substantially more than the first one.

Two pictures by a nonentity have now been sold in public for several thousands each (and, with any luck, the *Daily Telegraph* saleroom report has carried the headline: 'Record Price for Painting by A. Nonentity'). Others will now follow quickly (it is extraordinary how quickly numerous works by a newly-discovered moneymaker find their way into the sales). Little dealers all over the place are asking each other, 'Have you anything by Nonentity to sell?' Old-established and still old-fashioned dealers are scratching about in their stockrooms saying, 'I'm sure we used to have a couple of those bloody things.' Big boys in the Bond Street area are poised to move in on the Nonentity boom as soon as it looks big enough for their attention, and in no time one of them will be announcing an exhibition of 'Fine Paintings by A. Nonentity'. There will be a glossy, colour-illustrated catalogue (proceeds of sales to charity) with a foreword that discovers that the hitherto neglected Nonentity was a minor master (maybe not even 'minor'). By now, too, it will have been discovered that his brother, B. Nonentity, was almost as good an artist as himself and that his father, A. Nonentity Sen, wasn't bad either. In fact the whole Nonentity family for several generations were artists. Maybe there are (as with the felicitously named Koekkoek family) twenty or more of them, but, failing that, it is bound to be discovered that A. Nonentity had 'followers'. The ultimate accolade will come from some scruffy saleroom where terrible paintings that have nothing whatsoever to do with any of the twenty or more Nonentitys will be catalogued as 'School of Nonentity'.

In the ensuing scramble A. Nonentity's prices will escalate so rapidly that no one stops to look at the paintings, it is enough to see the price tag – £10,000! – It must be good. Then one day a painting by him that really is good turns up in a London sale. It is a large, museum-size canvas that he painted for love before he surrendered completely to the profitable production of potboilers for the fashionable trade of his day. Now, surely, even the aesthetically blind, money-orientated art speculators will see that they have paid ten times too much for most of the Nonentitys they have bought. This one is so much superior it could really be worth £5,000, which would make all the others worth around £500 to £1,000. But no, people with £10,000 tied up in A. Nonentity don't see it like that. At the sale the Nonentity 'masterpiece' (that is what it is being called already) fetches £35,000. No one notices or cares that this is more than the record price paid for a work by the seventeenth-century artist of whom A. Nonentity is a nineteenth-century imitator. Investors in Nonentity, his family, his followers or his 'school' go home happily and mark up the value of their investment by another 100 per cent.

Were this book simply an updated version of *The Art Game* I would feel obliged to tell you here the names of those artists whose identities are concealed behind the *nom de pinceau* 'A. Nonentity' so that you might jump on to their bandwagons. I would even feel that I had to name all those artists who, in my opinion, will be the Nonentitys of the future, so that you could put your money on them at the starting-price. But I so deplore this aspect of the art game that I cannot bring myself to do it. Of course my protest will have absolutely no effect, for many dealers have built up very successful businesses upon the sort of pictures I have in mind, Christie's have been holding special sales of them, under the title 'Narrative and Landscape Pictures', since 1965, and Sotheby's, who were a little slower off the mark, made up for their tardiness in 1973 by being the first to refer to them as 'Important Pictures'. But it was only the prices, not the pictures, that were important. Had Sothebys fallen into the same trap as the idiot brigade? Did they really believe that because the prices of pictures by nineteenth-century artists such as Springer, Leickert, Dommersen, Schelfhout, and Eversen, or Brunery, Croegart, and De Blaas (oh dear, I've let some of the cats out of the bag) were high the pictures must be 'important', or were they cunningly asserting the right of such pictures to take the place of the 'important' old masters that are now in such short supply?

Whatever the explanation, the prices paid today for paintings by derivative or simply decorative artists of no distinction underline the fact that there is no longer any sane relationship between prices and quality. Clearly fashion, always a factor in the art game, has in recent times become of overriding importance. As a result a new type of dealer, shrewder than those of the old brigade has emerged. Always alert for the first signs of a new trend in the taste of the undiscerning but well-heeled picture-buying public he quickly makes himself a corner in the embryo market and, with others of his kind, rapidly builds it up to a very profitable fashion.

Today, when the boom is so strong, we tend to overlook the possibility or, rather, the probability that most fashions will fade just as they always have done. The lifespan of a fashion is largely dependent upon the amount of money that is invested in it, especially the amount invested in it by the dealers. The dealer in fashionable artists knows well that 'prosperity crowns those who ride the waves of fashion with a timing nice enough to slip from one to another before each breaks.' This applies alike to long-dead or living artists who are suddenly rocketed into the sky-high brackets. In either case the investor-collector must cultivate the same degree of agility as the dealers if he is not to be left holding an unprofitable baby or two. But his only true safeguard will be to cultivate his taste so that he is attracted only to those few currently fashionable artists who have enduring qualities that justify the prices demanded for their works at the time he is buying. As we shall see in the next chapter, the investor-collector who develops such agility and has large funds to support his perceptiveness can make huge profits.

For the little man playing the lower level of the game it is clearly a great advantage to be able to detect as early as possible what the 'big boys' are up to. If he is a very shrewd little man he may even perceive what they are doing before they themselves know. Not long ago I was discussing with just such a shrewd little man, who sat beside me at Sotheby's, the remarkable way in which top prices for the works of such stolid pillars of 'modern' British painting as Gore, Gilman, Ginner, Bevan, Sickert, Roberts, had suddenly shot through the ten-thousand-pound barrier and were still rising. He was, he said, not the least surprised and claimed to have seen it coming as far back as 1964. That was the year, he explained, when the London Group celebrated its fiftieth anniversary with an exhibition at the Tate Gallery which brought together examples of the best of all the most significant groups of artists working in Britain during the first half of this century. He was so impressed that he began to make his own collection on the same lines and now has works by all the principal members of the Camden Town Group, of the Vorticists and English Futurists, and of our home-grown surrealists and pioneer abstractionists.

When I remarked that it was now too late for any but the rich to buy Camden Town paintings or works by the Vorticists, he pointed out that there were many minor members of the first group and a few of the second whose names were still hardly known, and that so far as the surrealists and abstractionists were concerned the game had hardly begun.* The list that follows includes all the names given to me by the 'shrewd little man' and a number of others chosen by me for no better reason than that I think they have some quality and are still sufficiently underpriced to make them fair short-term investments. Many of the latter have been associated with such groups as the New English or the Euston Road, some may even be or have been Academicians; it hardly matters and there is no need to classify them. But the Vorticists, Surrealists, and Abstractionists are marked (V) (Su) and (Abs) respectively. (Sc) denotes a sculptor.

Robert Adams (Sc)	Edward Bawden
Bernard Adeney	Keith Baynes
Eileen Agar (Su)	Graham Bell (Abs)
John Armstrong (Su)	John Selby Bigge (Su)
Laurence Atkinson (V)	Beatrice Bland
John Banting (Su)	Reginald Brill

*In March 1974 the Tate Gallery put on a display of 'abstract works of the thirties and forties by Moynihan. Morton, Vézelay, Wells, and Kenneth Martin'; Fischer Fine Art showed the surrealist works of Ceri Richards; and another dealer announced a show of Julian Trevelyan's surrealist paintings.

Thomas Carr (Abs)

Prunella Clough

Alan Clutton-Brock

Cecil Collins (Su)

Philip Connard

Raymond Coxon

Winifred Dacre (Abs)

R Poussette Dart (Abs)

Jessica Dismorr (V)

Frank Dobson (Sc)

John Dodgson (Su)

Malcolm Drummond

Alan Durst (Sc)

Florence Engelbach

Merlyn Evans (Su, Abs)

Frederick Etchells (V)

Jessie Etchells

Roger Furse

Roger Fry

Ethel Gabain

William Gear (Abs)

Sylvia Gosse

Wilhelmina Barns Graham (Abs)

Arthur Hacker

Sam Haile (Su)

Cuthbert Hamilton (V)*

Stanley W Hayter (Su, Abs)

Alfred Hayward

Adrian Heath (Abs)

Stanley Houghton

Charles Howard (Su, Abs)

Thelma Hulbert

Edgar Hubert (Abs)

Arthur Jackson (Abs)

Humphrey Jennings (Su, Abs)

E McKnight Kauffer (Su, Abs)

Mary Kessel

Maurice Kestelman

Jacob Kramer

Maurice Lambert (Sc)

Edward Le Bas

Louis Le Brocquy (Abs)

Therese Lessore

F E McWilliam (Sc, Su)

Conroy Maddox (Su)

Paul Maitland

J B Manson

Kenneth Martin (Abs)

Robert Medley (Su)

John Melville (Su)

Bernard Meninsky

E L T Mesens (Su)

Alastair Morton (Abs)

Marlow Moss (Abs, Sc)

Rodrigo Moynihan (Abs)

Grace Pailthorpe (Su)

Roland Penrose (Su)

*You will be lucky to find anything by Hamilton. Most of his Vorticist work has disappeared.

52

John Piper (Abs)

Frederick Porter

Mary Potter

Peter Potworowski

William Ratcliffe

Victor Reinganum (Su, Abs)

Ceri Richards (Su, Abs)

Edith Rimmington (Su)

Claude Rogers

Isaac Rosenberg

Helen Saunders (V)

Elliott Seabrooke

Dorothy Shakespear (V)

Bernhard Sickert

Ruskin Spear

J C Stephenson (Abs)

Walter Taylor

Geoffrey Tibble (Abs)

William Townsend

Julian Trevelyan (Su)

John Tunnard (Su, Abs)

Paule Vézelay (Abs)

Myerscough Walker (Su)

John Wells (Abs)

No aspect of the boom of recent years has been more spectacular than that of prints. The soaring prices in this field (according to an American art-index they rose by four hundred per cent in 1973 alone) are ominously reminiscent of those in the antique silver market before its near-collapse in the late sixties. The important works that now fetch enormous prices have dragged up behind them, into price brackets that have no justification, a huge variety of contemporary rubbish that is largely produced by mechanical, mass-production methods. Today, any artist whose paintings sell is likely to be invited by a publisher to produce an 'image' (as the current jargon goes) for a limited edition print. And because the publisher's profits are high the painter will probably find the fee irresistible, even though he has no experience of, talent for, or interest in printmaking. But before the spectre of big money corrupted artists things were very different.

Writing in 1929 in a special number of the *Studio* devoted to contemporary printmakers, William Gaunt noted that Great

Britain was the country where etching and engraving were most popular and most strongly cultivated as distinct branches of the arts. With unusual prescience he remarked that in the vogue it was then enjoying the etching, 'intimate, sometimes exquisite, easily understood . . . assumes also a speculative value – a condition of things similar to that which prevails on the Stock Exchange'. Well, like share certificates in 1929, those etchings were heading for a disastrous fall. Until very recently it was possible to buy prints by all the etchers and engravers praised by Gaunt for prices far lower than those they fetched in the 1920s. Even today, when it is virtually impossible to find any printmaker of quality whose work the present boom has completely overlooked, the prints of nearly all those fine craftsmen are still undervalued and are sure to rise as long as the boom continues.

In the list that follows I have added to the names of those I call 'Gaunt's Men' (and Women) the names of others, a few of them not British, whose prices in the salerooms still seem to me to be lagging. There are also those, like Sickert, John, Graham Sutherland, Muirhead Bone, Paul Nash, Edward Wadsworth whose prices, although already fairly high, are likely to go much higher:

S Van Abbé	Felix Bracquemond
Stanley Anderson	Leonard G Brammer
Robert Austin	Frank Brangwyn
S R Badmin	Arthur Briscoe
Marius A J Bauer	Gerald Brockhurst
Edward Bawden	John Buckland-Wright
Edmund Blampied	Enid Butcher
Douglas P Bliss	Charles W Cain
Muirhead Bone	D Y Cameron

Tom Chadwick
C S Cheston
Robert Colquhoun
Hermine David
Francis Dodd
Paul Drury
John Farleigh
H Andrew Freeth
Elizabeth Fyfe
Robert Gibbings
Eric Gill
Stephen Gooden
John F Greenwood
F L Griggs
Anthony Gross
Allan Gwynne-Jones
F Seymour Haden
A Hartley
Blair Hughes-Stanton
Augustus John
Laura Knight
Loxton Knight
Sydney Lee
Alphonse Legros
Clare Leighton
Elyse Lord
E S Lumsden
George Mackley
Iain MacNab
James McBey
D McCance

Frank C Medworth
Mortimer Menpes
Agnes Miller-Parker
William Morgan
Claude Muncaster
Paul Nash
C R W Nevinson
Job Nixon
J McIntosh Patrick
Claughton Pellew
Joseph Pennell
R C Peter
G Spencer Pryse
Gwen Raverat
Eric Ravilious
Henry Rushbury
Randolph Schwabe
Claude Shepperson
Frank Short
Joseph Simpson
D I Smart
Percy J Smith
Leonard Squirrel
Ian Strang
William Strang
Graham Sutherland
A R Middleton Todd
Julian Trevelyan
C F Tunnicliffe
Francis Unwin
Edward Wadsworth

William Walcot	John Wheatley
Charles J Watson	W L Wyllie
Clifford Webb	

For more than twenty years the firm of Abbot & Holder, operating in the London suburb of Barnes, have been successfully undercutting the snob dealers a few miles away in Mayfair in the thriving market for English watercolours and drawings. Since it has always been their purpose to cater for the small collector I asked them what there could possibly be in their field for such a man or woman in these days. They produced the following lists from which, in 1973, it had been possible for a collector with only £500 a year to spend to buy a dozen or more items.

First a list of amateurs of English Watercolours in the eighteenth and early nineteenth centuries (plus two of the professionals who taught them – Amos Green and Malchair):

John White Abbott	George Frost of Ipswich
Earl of Aylesford	Rev William Gilpin
(Heneage Finch)	Amos Green
Countess of Aylesford	Mrs Amos Green
Coplestone Warre Bampfylde	(Harriet Lister)
Lady Diana Beauclerk	George Heriot
Sir George Beaumont	Peter Richard Hoare
Rev William Bree	Sir Richard Colt Hoare
Dr William Crotch	J B Malchair
Rev John Eagles	Dr Thomas Monro
Sir Bulteel Fisher	Ker Porter
John Fisher, Bishop of	Sir James Steuart
Salisbury	Thomas Sunderland
Hon Henrietta Fortescue	Rev Joseph Wilkinson

Second, eighteen nineteenth-century artists who liked to make watercolours of historical subjects:

Sir William Boxall, RA	Sir J D Linton
C F Buckley	J Seymour Lucas, RA
Charles Cattermole	A D McCormick
George Cattermole	H Stacy Marks, RA
Ernest Croft, RA	Edith Martineau
Sir Frank Dicksee, RA	Samuel Rayner
W E Frost	Fredk Coke Smith
Sir John Gilbert	Francis P Stephanoff
Sir George Hayter	Frederick Weekes

Third, some illustrators, all famous in their day:

H M Bateman	Sir Bernard Partridge
C E Brock	G J Pinwell
H M Brock	Frank Reynolds
Hablot K Browne	Charles Robinson
Edmund Dulac	W Heath Robinson
George du Maurier	Harry Rountree
Charles Keene	Edmund J Sullivan
John Leech	Hugh Thomson
Phil May	

Finally Abbott & Holder gave me a list of some of *Les Élèves Chez Julian,* the name given by Lucien Pissarro to those British artists (and two Frenchmen who chose to work in Britain) who studied at the Académie Julian in Paris at the end of the last century. Even bearing in mind that we are still talking of watercolours and drawings, it is remarkable that a selection of as many as a dozen items by these artists could be bought for £500 in 1973:

Robert Anning Bell, RA

Hugh Bellingham-Smith

James Charles

George Clausen, RA

Sir Alfred East, RA

Mark Fisher, RA

Stanhope Forbes, RA

Elisabeth Stanhope Forbes

Roger Fry

Fred Hall

W Lee Hankey

Sir H Hughes-Stanton, RA

F W Jackson

Alphonse Legros

Jules Lessore

D S MacColl

A Winter Shaw

P Wilson Steer

Edward Stott, RA

Henry Tonks

H S Tuke, RA

Abbott & Holder stress that these lists are intended for genuine collectors, not 'investment-mongers'. But what art gamesman will let such nice, old-fashioned sentiments like that deter him from using the lists if there's a profit in them?

4

American Moneymakers

European painting is studied and tired, missing the freshness of spring. American painting bursts forth from the ground like flowers, disengaged from tradition and the past. If a man moves by plane rather than oxcart, why must he prefer Rubens to Pollock?

PHILIPPE DOTREMONT, *quoted in Time,* 11 August, 1961

As a European collector M Philippe Dotrement, the Belgian industrialist, was a rarity in the 1950s and 1960s. His attitude to contemporary American art was shared by few collectors on this side of the Atlantic. While many artists in Europe readily acknowledged the importance of the American art revolution of those decades, those Europeans who made a habit of backing their beliefs in art with money were much slower to be convinced. This had little, if anything, to do with chauvinism. It was primarily a matter of Old World conservatism coupled with the popularly held opinion that all Americans were crazy anyway.

Even after several years of domination of European painting by American painting, most European – and especially British – collectors (and dealers, too) still nursed the idea that the 'New American Painting' was a flash in the pan. They were suspicious of the way in which art was promoted in the United States and were unable to free themselves from the conviction that only cheapjack products are sold by cheapjack methods. For the most part their attitude to their American counterparts was that of indulgent parents to wayward children. They smiled a superior smile and thought, 'Let them get on with it. They'll learn in time.'

In the autumn of 1965, the superior smile became a guffaw when *Life International* magazine featured Mr and Mrs Robert C Scull in an article on Pop art headed, 'If You Buy It, How Do You Live With It?'. The illustrations showed Mr Scull apparently breakfasting on grapefruit and *vin rosé* while seated against a background of a highly indigestible sixteen-foot painting by James Rosenquist, and Mr and Mrs Scull posing like gourmets in front of a Claes Oldenburg stove laden with painted plaster food. The text quoted Mr Scull as saying that when he bought the Rosenquist in 1962 for $1,400 the artist stood and looked at him in astonishment and then said, 'I didn't think there'd be anyone crazy enough to buy it.'

Rosenquist's opinion of Skull's sanity must have been shared by the great majority of those who read that article, but later events showed that businessman Scull was several jumps ahead of us all. In order to make room in his life for his increasing collection of Pop works (including a second Rosenquist, 85 feet long and $60,000 high) he had disposed of thirteen paintings by De Kooning, Kline, Newman, Rothko, Still, and other contemporary American artists of a generation senior to the Pop boys. It was these pictures that came up for sale on 13 October 1965, at New York's Parke-Bernet Galleries, which had just become affiliated with Sotheby's of London.

The catalogue of this sale was a monument to Mr Scull's far-sightedness as a collector-investor. In almost every case the entries pertaining to his pictures included lists of impressive exhibitions to which the pictures had been lent. It would be invidious to suggest that in generously lending his treasured possessions to public exhibitions Mr Scull was influenced by the fact that it would add to their value when he came to sell them. But the fact remains that it did just that. Significantly, the most exhibited work in the sale, Willem de Kooning's *Police Gazette,* made the highest price $37,000. A Clyfford Still made $29,000, a Newman $26,000, and a Mark Tobey $14,000. But, viewed from London, the most remarkable price of the sale was $20,000 for a Pop picture, Robert Rauschenberg's chaotic combine painting, *Express.* This picture was not from the Scull collection, but its price gave him high hopes of the investment prospects of the pictures he still had at home.

But what exactly where those prospects? Two other New York collectors of Pop, interviewed by *Life,* gave diametrically opposite views. Mr Leonard Kraushar, who owned a Tom Wesselman *Great American Nude,* a stack of Andy Warhol's 'Brillo' boxes, and Claes Oldenburg's *Big Baked Potato,* held that 'Pop is the art of today, and tomorrow, and all the future.' Unlike other art, which was for old ladies, Pop would never die, he said. But Mr Harry Abrams was more realistic. He thought that Pop artists were giving us a new way of looking at things and, maybe, changing our whole idea of what con-stitutes taste. But he added, 'Before we know it, they'll be the old ones and we'll be on to something else.'

In Britain this more wary attitude to the latest art kick prevailed over all others. What Americans were calling their 'Vanguard Audience' had only a very feeble counterpart in Britain. Conditioned for so long to the idea that France was the birthplace of all modern art and would continue to be so for ever and ever, the British found it almost impossible to believe even in their own modern artists until (as in the cases of Henry Moore and Francis Bacon) they were acclaimed by other countries. It was hardly surprising, then, that such manifestations of the great American art revolution as appeared in the London salerooms in the early sixties called forth little covetousness in the bosoms of British collectors. For a short time it was possible to snap up an occasional bargain here, ship it straight to Parke-Bernet in New York, and at least double your money. But by 1965 no vendor in his right senses was likely to send a modern American painting of any importance to the London salerooms. This state of affairs continued right up to 1973 (but more of that later).

What were regarded here as the outrageous prices charged by American dealers for modern American art must have deterred even those British collectors who liked it or who were clever enough to see that, although they hated it, it might be a good investment. But it was not only the big price that was off-putting. The big format, too, was alien to the British collector. He equated it with the boastfulness and ostentatiousness of what he believed was the typical American, a big man with a big cigar in his big mouth, riding in an absurdly big car. There was also a much deeper reason. The British were not converted to the American craving for the new. It was to come, of course, as every bad American influence – from commercial television to drug-taking and from Woolworth's oil paintings to sex mania – has come. With increased affluence we, too, were ready to embrace the trade-it-in-throw-it-away philosophy which kept the wheels of the United States' never-never economy turning. We, too, came to believe that we must have the newest model car, television, refrigerator, washing-machine; so why not the newest model art?

In the past art collectors who spent large sums of money were very cautious about the new. They waited for the worth of new developments in art to be assessed by the critics and proved by time. But suddenly newness itself had a big price tag. In an essay, 'The New as Value', included in his book *The Anxious Object,* published 1968, the American art critic, Harold Rosenberg, explained how this came about. 'Novelties in painting and sculpture receive notice in the press as new *facts* long before thay have qualified as new *art'*, he says. He argues that once sufficient public attention has been drawn, by what-ever means, to a novel work, the critics are bound to take notice of it. And not only to take notice of it, but to approve of it, because 'to deny the significance of the new product begins to seem futile, since whatever is seen and talked about is already on its way to becoming a *fait accompli* of taste'. From there the work will be 'nudged into art history' and 'through attaining this place the work's own qualities become part of the standards by which the work is judged.'

I was reminded, by this description of the farce to which the business of art in America had descended, of the hoaxer who, in my youth, delivered a lecture to a learned society on 'the new philosophy, in which effect precedes cause'. But the situation in American art in the mid-sixties was obviously not going to be a short-term joke. You may have felt then that the whole damn lot of modern American art should be dumped in Central Park and burned, but already huge sums of money (and many huge reputations) had been staked upon its enduring qualities as a good investment.

The fact that works by many of the artists concerned were already in the permanent collections of great museums of modern art would, in other, soberer times have made those artists fairly safe long-term bets for collectors. But the processes by which so many of such works had found their way into the museums gave no such assurance. Describing those processes Mr Rosenberg wrote:

> Reputations are now being made in art as fast as on Broadway and in Hollywood. The past few seasons have provided the spectacle of museum personnel, critics, and professors of current art history being swept up in a race to identify themselves with half-emerged personalities and trends; curators touring the country as advance agents for exhibitions of neo-this or that; public and private buyers acquiring collections that amount to kits made of the latest names; university instructors playing the part of sideshow-barkers in front of the slides flipped through their projection machines . . The speed-up in history-making has now reached the point where the interval of critical evaluation seems to have become superfluous.*

I was once told by the director of a major public gallery of modern art that his job was not to create a collection of great or even good art but only to make sure that the collection reflected what was going on in art. Now even that aim has been abandoned by many people in positions such as his (including his successor). Lack of conviction that much of the art of today is, in fact, art at all has forced them to leave such judgment to posterity. But for the private investor-collector this is not good enough.

*Harold Rosenberg, *op cit.*

Most art museum basements are stacked with works that were once highly prized, then despised, but all, it seems, have made or will make at least a partial comeback in the avidly revivalist art world of today. The mass of modern American art in museums will also, presumably, be subject some day to this appreciation-contempt-reappraisal cycle. Indeed, since everything in life has been speeded up enormously in recent times, we might reasonably have expected Pop and its antecedents to have arrived at the contempt stage already. Not at all. At a sale of *Contemporary Art, 1945-1973* held in London by Sotheby's July 1973, prices for a number of American works were high, and although many of the buyers came from abroad there were signs of some interest among British collectors. A gigantic Warhol banality, *Flowers,* 120 in by 120 in, fetched £24,000. Yet most of the London prices were soon shown to be bargain prices when, in October the same year, Mr Scull decided to see once again how his investments had done. Even he must have been surprised by the monstrous (I choose the word deliberately) prices they fetched. The sale at the Parke-Bernet Galleries totalled £923,000 ($2,242,900) for fifty lots. The highest price and the craziest price were each paid for works by Jasper Johns. His encaustic and collage map of the USA – title *Double White Map,* 90 in by 70 in – made £98,765 ($240,000); his notorious *Painted Bronze* – a couple of realistic replicas in bronze of a Ballantine ale can – went for £37,037 ($90,000). De Kooning's *Police Gazette,* evidently the same painting as that knocked down at $37,000 (presumably bought in!) at Mr Scull's sale of 1965 realised £74,074 ($180,000). A very large Barnett Newman abstraction of 1960, *White Fire II,* fetched £63,786 ($155,000); a huge, typical Franz Kline, *Orange and Black Wall,* £51,440 ($125,000). A Warhol *Flowers,* slightly less gigantic (but no less banal) than the one sold in London, fetched £55,555 ($135,000).

The London *Flowers* was entirely blue, the New York one multi-coloured. A case of penny plain, tuppence coloured. There was no such simple explanation, however, for the curious difference in price of two Warhol *Campbell's Soup Can* paintings. Although identical in size and every detail (except that the first was a *beef* soup can, the second a *tomato* one), the price in London was £7,000, that in New York only £4,940 ($12,000).

The art market of today is so different from that of even ten years ago that, looking back, I am amazed at the temerity with which I made forecasts in *The Art Game.* To predict the course a fashion will take and to estimate how long it will last is now a job for an actuary with a computer. So much money is now invested in art that one fashion will not be allowed to give way gracefully to the next. Indeed, it may well be that the ability of a fashion to survive is in direct proportion to the amount of money invested in it. And for this reason, although Americans are notoriously fickle, the fashion among American art collectors for the new American Vanguard art (as they like to call it) may be expected to break records for longevity. Another reason is that American art pundits cannot agree with M Dotremont's view that disengagement from tradition is a virtue. They hunger for a tradition that they can call their own and see abstract expressionism and Pop as the beginnings of that tradition. If and when any reappraisal does come it is unlikely to be allowed to alter the status in American art-history books of twentieth-century 'old masters' such as Jackson Pollock (whose *Blue Poles* was bought by the Australian National Gallery for £800,000 in 1973), Mark Rothko, Willem de Kooning, Franz Kline, and Barnett Newman. And only over the dead bodies of many millionaire investor-collectors is it likely to be allowed to diminish the standing (bought at a cost of millions of dollars) of the next batch in the history books – Johns, Warhol, Rauschenberg, Lichtenstein, Rosenquist & Co.

For the present, then, the investment value of American Vanguard Art has nothing to do with whether it is great art, or whether it is art at all. It has to do only with how long the fad (the word is Warhol's, not mine) can be kept going. It may seem to you that prices have already gone so absurdly high that they cannot possibly go any higher, but I have made the mistake of thinking that many times in the past. Now I have learned that the higher the price the better investment it will appear to the idiot brigade (whose biggest membership is in America). So if you have the right sort of money to buy yourself a portrait of a soup tin, a joint of painted-plaster meat or a couple of (empty) bronze beer cans, go ahead and do it. If you are an American you can get a tax rebate by promising your treasure to a museum, where it will be preserved for centuries as a curious manifestation of a mad period in which the more artists themselves railed against the old art values and thumbed their noses at the collectors and the experts, the wider those collectors and experts spread their arms to receive the material expressions of their abuse. And paid big money for the privilege of doing so. In such an opportunist's heaven it is, surely, too much to expect any artist to keep his integrity, and utterly ingenuous to expect to find any great art.

5

Let The Buyer
Still Beware

*Each and every statement in Christie's Catalogues, Advertisements
or Brochures of forthcoming sales as to any Lot is made without
responsibility on the part of Christie's or the Seller of that lot.*

Notice in all Christie's sale catalogues.

No auctioneer likes having to say caveat emptor. *But he will if he
has to.*

JOHN CARTER, *The Auction Room* (1958)

One result of writing *The Art Game* was that I was frequently
accosted in the London salerooms (and twice even in the
Parke-Bernet Galleries in New York) by complete strangers.
Without exception they said a few polite words about the book
and then proceeded to tell me some experience of their own
that I ought to have included in it. Within a few months I had
heard enough stories to fill another volume. Most of them came
from newcomers to the art game (several admitted to having
started playing as a result of reading the book) who were still

pop-eyed at the little fiddles that to experienced players are so commonplace that they don't even provoke a raised eyebrow.

Many of the tales concerned the sudden appearance of signatures on paintings by artists who had been dead fifty, one hundred, two hundred and more years. A similar number told of paintings, first seen in one junk sale, turning up in another a few weeks later with the labels of reputable galleries stuck on their backs. One concerned the disappearance during the preview at a minor London saleroom, of a genuine certificate of authenticity attached to the back of a genuine painting by Monticelli.

But the most interesting of these stories came from a young American who had bought, for ten pounds in a London street market, a lithograph bearing a spurious monogram of Maillol. When his mistake was pointed out to him he went to the police-station nearest to the street market and reported that a crime had been perpetrated in the parish. His confidence in the excellence of British Justice led him to believe that swift action would be taken and he would recover his ten pounds. But the police told him they could do nothing. He would have to take legal action through the courts, they said. This would cost a lot of money and the most he could hope to get back would be his ten pounds, so they advised him to forget it.

Instead, the young man went back to the street-trader, accused him of selling a fake and demanded his money back. The trader gladly paid up remarking as he did so that he could easily sell the lithograph again – he had already sold two like it that morning. But that was by no means the end of the story. Having had his fingers burned the American determined that it should not happen again. From that day he spent most of his spare time studying prints and quickly acquired an impressive knowledge of their technical aspects, but he had still to develop the feeling by which to distinguish good drawing from bad. This led him once to buy a 1920s fake set of Wheatley's ubiquitous *Cries of London,* printed on simulated eighteenth-century watermarked paper but so badly drawn that one would have thought even a child could see it. And when he ventured for the first time to buy (in Los Angeles!) old English water-colours, he landed himself with a pair of amateurishly fake Rowlandsons.

Later he paid a Bond Street antiques dealer £850 for what appeared to be Daumier's bronze, *Le Ratapoil* (one such had been sold at Parke-Bernet's a few weeks earlier for $24,000) only to discover that it was three inches shorter than it ought to have been. But that time he had no hesitation in demanding his money back – and got it – for only two months before, on 22 April 1967, the Misrepresentation Act had come into force.

The position legally obtaining in England before the act came into force was well publicised in 1966 when Mr Harry Spiro, a New Orleans collector who had bought a fake Renoir at Christie's in 1963, succeeded in getting his three-year-old story into the *New York Times.* To most people, who were unaware of the legal position, it made very curious reading. The *New York Times* article, amusingly written by the paper's art critic, John Canaday, is worth quoting in full:

THE LOST INNOCENCE OF MR BADDLEIGH TAKEN

This is the story of Mr Baddleigh Taken and the firm of Starction's a contraction of Standard Art Auctions. It is a true story, although the names are invented.

The protagonists must be introduced:
Starction's is one of the oldest and most respected art auction

houses in the world. So much for Starction's. Mr Taken cannot be described so briefly. He is an American collector, new at the game, whose first purchases were made only a couple of years ago. Not quite within hailing distance of middle age, but already possessed of considerable means, he decided to enlarge his life by extending his interests seriously into culture – an admirable project. He not only began buying art but also demonstrated his public spirit by establishing a foundation to bring art scholars to his city to lecture. (The latter aspect of Mr Taken's cultural adventures does not concern us here, since so far it has not run him into any interesting trouble.)

Mr Taken has been busily educating himself in the subtle field of aesthetics and art history, but – with no pretentions to scholarship as yet – he is still at that stage of the game where his first faith must remain in the dependability of familiar name-products. He will buy a Renoir on faith because he knows Renoir to have been a good artist and because as a businessman he has learned that the law of supply and demand can be trusted when the supply is curtailed (Renoir is dead) and the demand is giltedged (museums want Renoir). But he is still a long way, for example, from knowing that if you can find a drawing indisputably from the hand of Primaticcio you have a treasure. He would not recognise such a drawing at an auction and might wonder why the bidding was so lively among dealers. But if he still has a lot to learn about art, he has learned one thing about art auctions, which is that you are a sitting duck if you expect them to operate within the most delicate nuances of good faith between buyer and seller.

That is how he got into trouble at Starction's.

A few months after he began collecting, Mr Taken, who had yet to be taken, had every reason to believe that he could trust the combination of the names Renoir and Starction, and in his faith he bid on a pastel listed as Renoir's in the advance catalogue of a Starction auction. To his delight he got the picture, at a price somewhat above $7,000 – a bargain, which might have made him suspicious in the first place, since bargains come up in art auctions hardly more frequently than hens' teeth.

But after he got his picture home his delight began to wane. He could not make it look just right, an indication that his sensibilities were already becoming dependable. He took the picture to New York for examination by an undisputed authority on Impressionist painting, who said that in his opinion there was not a chance in the world that it was a real Renoir, and that he would testify in court if asked.

Mr Taken got in touch with Starction's. He wanted his money back, and had no doubt at all that Starction's would shoot him a refund. It seemed reasonable to him that Starction's would no more want to sell him a bad painting for a good cheque than that he would want to pay Starction's with a bad cheque for a good painting. He even thought that Starction's would be embarrassed by their *faux pas.*

Starction's didn't see it that way at all.

The transaction had been completed, and as far as they were concerned that was the end of it. If Mr Taken wanted to sue the seller, that was all right with them. But by the standard terms of sale, an auction house is not the seller but only the intermediary agent, between seller and buyer, with no responsibility whatsoever for attributions, authenticity, representations, faults, imperfections, inaccurate descriptions or anything else except the mechanics of the change of hands, which Starction's had accomplished.

Mr Taken could not understand this. He felt that the good name of a business house must depend upon guaranteed merchandise. But he had no legal means of redress. In the auction business, even at topmost levels, there are no regulations corresponding to, say, the pure food laws. And although auction houses sometimes withdraw a fake upon discovery, and sometimes make restitution to a purchaser, whether or not they do so is entirely up to them.

All of this was distressing enough to Mr Taken, but his indignation (and incredulity) mounted upon further discussion with Starction's. Starction's had not simply made an embarrassing error. When the picture came in for sale, they told him, they had held no doubts as to its authenticity, but, like Mr Taken later on, they had begun to have their doubts while the picture was on the walls. Their opinion had become that it was probably a fake, but they had allowed it to go on the block as a Renoir anyway. The only comfort they offered Mr Taken was their assurance that they still felt a residual hope to the extent of twenty per cent (a curious calculation) that the picture was genuine. After all, Starction's said, fakes are difficult to distinguish from the real thing under certain circumstances. As to the signature, they said cheerfully, but to Mr Taken's way of thinking not to much point, that if the signature was not Renoir's it had been forged with exceptional skill.

Mr Taken was not interested in collecting examples of the forger's skill, and he wondered what disposition could be made of the picture to recoup at least a portion of its cost. And now he was truly and completely appalled by Starction's advice. It would be unwise to put the picture up for public sale right away, they cautioned him. Dealers would remember it, question so quick an offering of it for resale, and murder it by grapevine. Mr Taken was advised to get rid of the picture privately (presumably by fobbing it off on another collector as innocent as he had been before this experience) or to sit on it long enough so that its reappearance would not seem suspicious. Here Mr Taken touched bottom, feeling that the insult of invitation to perpetuate a fraud had been added to the injury of having been the original victim.

There are various ways of reading this story. It has been told from Mr Taken's point of view, although not with the passionate eloquence to which it inspires him. At the opposite point of view, perhaps Starction's the argument could be that an art auction house is a different thing entirely from an art dealer, subject to none of the obligations upon which a dealer's good name depends, and that anyone unwilling to accept the risks involved and not yet be an expert judge of what is offered for sale, has no business being in the auction room and must settle for licking his own wounds upon leaving the arena. From either point of view, the story of this little transaction is only the slightest footnote to a situation that is rooted in the art auction boom and spreads its ramifications to affect areas as diverse as the Federal tax laws and our esthetic standards.*

Some time after that article appeared (unknown to me), Mr Spiro (also unknown to me) wrote a letter outlining his story and enclosing photostat copies of all the correspondence in the case. He had, he said, just read *The Art Game* and thought that I might be able to help him recover his money. In the event of his being successful he would donate the whole sum to provide a scholarship for a British art student to study in the United States. Without much conviction I advised Mr Spiro to tell his story to the *Sunday Times,* which, not long before, had done a remarkable job in exposing the activities of an antiques auction ring. A few months later, to my great surprise, that paper came out with the whole story. No pseudonyms were used. A spade was a spade, Spiro was Spiro and Christie's was Christie's.

During the months before the act became law, anticipation of what it might do to the art trade turned many a dealer and auctioneer into a manic-depressive. Many people (including me) who ought to have known better had, for some reason that now seems ridiculous, come to believe that the act was going to bring dramatic changes to the art trade, that it would end for ever the iniquitous old legal let-out of *caveat emptor* (let the

*John Canaday in *The New York Times,* 16 January 1966

75

buyer beware) and so bring about a dramatic cleaning-up process in the art trade. Shady dealers and men with little or no knowledge who had gone into art simply because it was booming, must, we believed, have been trembling at the thought of what might happen to their rackets. Reputable dealers, whose reputations depend upon their readiness to guarantee the things they sell, were however more concerned with its effect upon the salerooms than upon themselves. They reasoned that if, as a result of the act, auctioneers were obliged to give a guarantee to every buyer (as is the case in France) then the number of private buyers at pictures sales (already much greater than it had been a decade earlier) was likely to be vastly increased and the dealers would lose customers.

At the time (6 December 1963) when Mr Spiro had bought his 'Renoir', Christie's were legally protected by a 'disclaimer clause', No 5 in their 'Conditions of Sale' which appeared in all their catalogues:

> *The lots to be taken away and paid for, whether genuine and authentic or not, with all faults and errors of description, at the Buyer's expense and risk within TWO DAYS from the Sale; Messrs Christie, Manson and Woods, Ltd, not being responsible for the correct description, genuineness, or authenticity of, or any fault or defect in, any Lot, and making no warranty whatsoever.*

Curiously this clause, unlike the corresponding one in Sotheby's 'Conditions of Sale', did not protect the seller of the picture and, therefore, Mr Spiro could have sued the vendor. But when, at his request, Christie's revealed that the vendor was a Frenchwoman living in Paris he decided that to launch such a lawsuit from his home, 4,000 miles away in New Orleans, against someone in France might easily prove more expensive that his original mistake.

In 1965, by which time Mr Spiro had abandoned his direct appeals to the auctioneers, Christie's expanded their 'disclaimer clause' to cover the sellers of goods:

5 *(a)* *Each Lot is sold by the Seller thereof with all faults and defects therein and with all errors of description and is to be taken and paid for whether genuine and authentic or not and no compensation shall be paid for the same.*

  (b) *Christie, Manson & Woods Ltd, act as agents only and are not responsible for the correct description, genuineness nor authenticity of nor any fault nor defect in any Lot and make no warranty whatsoever.*

But it was not until 1967, after the Misrepresentation Act had become law, that Christie's gave any sort of guarantee against the type of misfortune that Mr Spiro had suffered. Then this clause appeared in their catalogues of picture sales:

6. *Notwithstanding any other terms of these Conditions, if within 21 days after the sale a Buyer of any Lot returns the same to CHRISTIE, MANSON & WOODS LTD in the same condition as at the time of the sale and satisfies CHRISTIE, MANSON & WOODS LTD that considered in the light of the entry in the Catalogue the Lot is a deliberate forgery then the sale of the Lot will be rescinded and the purchase price of the same refunded.*

In fact, even if Christie's had been giving this 'guarantee' in 1963 it might not have saved the situation for Mr Spiro, because it was more than a month before he was able to inform Christie's that a New York expert had pronounced his picture a fake.

The reason for the three weeks' limit is that up to that time the whole of the money paid by the buyers in the saleroom is still in the hands of the auctioneers, the settlement with the sellers usually being made after a month. Sotheby's, who introduced a similar clause into their Old Master sale catalogues at about the same time, had had a much more satisfactory clause in their conditions for sales of 'Modern British' and 'Impressionist and Modern' paintings, drawings, and sculpture, since 1962. In these cases the reference is not to 'forgery' but to 'serious doubt as to the authenticity of the lot', a term of much wider significance. If, for example, I were to buy an unsigned *pointilliste* painting which is catalogued as by Seurat but which turns out to be by the minor artist, Charles Angrand, I cannot claim that I have bought a forgery, but I can claim that there is serious doubt as to the authenticity of my 'Seurat'.

Another apparent effect of the Misrepresentation Act upon the major auction houses was their decision to publish an explanation of the 'code' used in cataloguing. In all their catalogues of paintings, drawings, prints and miniatures, Christie's announce:

Terms used in this catalogue have the meanings ascribed to them below:—

The first name or names and surname of the artist –	*In our opinion a work by the artist*
The initials of the first name(s) and the surname of the artist –	*In our opinion a work of the period of the artist and which may be in whole or part the work of the artist*
The surname only of the artist –	*In our opinion a work of the school or by one of the followers of the artist or in his style*
The surname of the artist preceded by 'After'	*In our opinion a copy of the work of the artist*

'(*)'	*This indicates that the convential term in this Glossary is not appropriate but that in our opinion the work is a work by the artist named*
'Signed'	*Has a signature which in our opinion is the signature of the artist*
'Bears signature'	*Has a signature which in our opinion might be the signature of the artist*
'Dated'	*Is so dated and in our opinion was executed at about that date.*
'Bears date'	*Is so dated and in our opinion may have been executed at about that date.*

Sotheby's, whose glossary of terms is similar, differ from Christie's in that they do not publish the glossary in the catalogues of 'Impressionist and Modern' and 'Modern British' sales. The reason for this is that in these types of sale they will include only works which can in their opinion or that of any expert they may consult, be definitely attributed to a particular artist. (In 1973, alas, Sotheby's slackened this excellent rule and began to include in their 'Modern British' sales works which were cautiously described as 'School of Sickert', 'Sir W Orpen, attributed to' etc).

Years before these 'glossaries' began to appear in saleroom catalogues, I had drawn attention to the existence and meaning of the codes, first in newspaper articles and then, at some length, in *The Art Game,* and was not surprised to find that many people who regularly frequented the salerooms did not understand them. Sotheby's and Christie's lead in publishing their cataloguing codes was soon followed by other auctioneers in London and all over the country. But praiseworthy as the idea was, it created a problem for the great majority of the minor auction houses, few of whom could honestly claim to have anyone on their staffs qualified to have any opinion on the attributions of works of art. The solution for many of these firms was a drastic decrease in the number of artists' names appearing in their catalogues and a proliferation of such terms as 'style of', 'manner of', 'Dutch school', '19th Century English', '17th Century Italian' and so on. One auctioneer in the south of England invented an entirely new term to meet what he thought were the requirements of the Misrepresentation Act.

My first acquaintance with this firm came in 1965 when one of its very fat catalogues dropped uninvited through my letterbox. A quick flick through its pages revealed a list of artists' names of which Sotheby's would have been proud. Many of the names were misspelled, and, although I ought to have known better I, found such teasers as 'R Picasso', 'Berth Morrisot', 'Roual Dufy', 'Simon Solomons', 'Fueline' and 'R McNeil Whistler' irresistible. I made a round trip of 200 miles to view.

I was particularly anxious to see a painting catalogued as 'D Bomberg', a pencil and chalk drawing entered as 'E L Kirchner (1880-1938)', a watercolour 'sketch of two mythical horses' listed as 'J de Chirico', a pen and ink sketch under the name 'Marini', and another signed 'H Matisse', and several works given simply as 'Sisley'.

I need hardly tell how it turned out. The 'R Picasso' certainly had nothing to do with Pablo of the same surname, while 'Simon Solomons' seemed more likely to be related to the well-known Jack greengrocer-boxing-promoter-bookmaker

Solomons than to the artist Simeon Solomon. The 'Berth Morissot' was not to be confused in any way with Berthe Morisot. The work listed as 'Fueline' and described as a 'pen and ink engraving', was an engraving after Fuseli. 'R McNeil Whistler' must have been an extremely remote relative, if any, of Jimmy McNeill Whistler. The 'D Bomberg' was evidently the work of one of those painting chimpanzees, masquerading under a famous name. In spite of the 'documents' stuck to its reverse side to prove the contrary, the 'E L Kirchner' had no resemblance whatsoever to the work of Ernst Ludwig of that name, and the 'watercolour' by 'J de Chirico' was, in fact, a tattered reproduction of a well-known painting by Giorgio de Chirico. And so on with most of the 'modern works' in the sale.

It was obvious that whoever did the cataloguing knew virtually nothing about modern pictures and I was, at first, very puzzled as to how he had decided upon the names he had put on them. Then I turned some of the pictures over and found that in most cases where the picture itself did not bear a false signature a name had been scribbled on the back, always in the same bold hand, and that this name had been used in the catalogue. It seemed reasonable to conclude that these 'attributions' were made by a (to put it kindly) optimistic and ignorant vendor and followed by a (to put it kindly, again) naïve cataloguer.

This firm's catalogues continued to drop through my letter-box at regular intervals for two or three years and provided me with some amusing reading. Sometimes the temptation to go to view the sale, just to see what was behind some particularly intriguing description of a lot, was almost too much for me but I resisted. How, I wondered one day after 22 April 1967, would this particular firm meet the challenge of the

Misrepresentation Act. I had not long to wait. The following month another fat catalogue arrived. There were noticeably fewer 'big names' in it than in its forerunners and most of those that did appear were followed by the words 'After by' in brackets – Hogarth (After by), Wilson (After by), and so on. But whatever modifications the smaller salerooms made in their cataloguing, the fact was, and still is, that ninety-nine per cent of such firms employ no one qualified to make attributions of any sort. If they cared at all about sticking to the law they would have to apply the old army maxim, 'No names, no packdrill'.

Now that the Misrepresentation Act has been in force for many years the initial fear of it has long been forgotten and only the bigger salerooms make any serious attempt to comply with it. The reason is that, like the 'anti-rings' act of 1927 (under which, I believe, not a single successful prosecution has ever been made), the Misrepresentation Act 1967 is full of loopholes for an offending vendor or auctioneer. The act was widely expected to invalidate the preposterous 'disclaimer clause' that is universal among English auctioneers, but after saying (in Section 3) that any such provision for 'excluding liability for misrepresentation' shall be of no effect, the act continues, 'except to the extent (if any) that, in any proceedings arising out of the contract, the court or arbitrator may allow reliance on it as being fair and reasonable in the circumstances of the case.' So the disclaimer clause stays in the catalogues.

Another, even more glaring, example of the Act pulling out its own teeth before they had a chance to bite comes in Section 2, which is headed 'Damages for Misrepresentation'. This begins by saying that if you or I (or Mr Spiro) have bought a Renoir (or such-and-such) which isn't a Renoir (or such-and-such) and as a result have suffered loss, then, 'if the person making the misrepresentation would be liable to damages in respect thereof had the misrepresentation been made fraudulently, *that person shall be so liable notwithstanding* that the misrepresentation was not made fraudulently . . .'

Good, you say. Quite right. A buyer should be given what he pays for or get his money back if he is given the wrong thing by mistake. But hold on a moment. Here comes the teeth extraction! The clause continues: ' . . . unless he proves that he had reasonable ground to believe and did believe up to the time the contract was made that the facts represented were true.'

How asinine can the law get? Here we have what is nothing short of discrimination in favour of the ignorant and dishonest and against the knowledgeable and honest. If, as can and does sometimes happen, a fake is sold as genuine at one of the major salerooms, where a genuine effort is made by, or with the help of, experts to ensure authenticity, then testimony by those experts that they believed up to the time of the sale that the work was genuine would result in either

(a) the truthfulness of their testimony being questioned, or

(b) their prestige as experts suffering a blow.

Whatever testimony those experts give will, to some extent, damage the firm's reputation. If only because of this, then, the reputable firms have had reason to increase their vigilance as a result of the Misrepresentation Act. But those auctioneers who, through ignorance or dishonesty, accept the spurious attributions given to pictures by vendors, have virtually nothing to lose. If charged with misrepresentation they could argue that they had not the necessary knowledge to doubt the attribution of the picture as it was given to them by the vendor. Which brings us to the question of the auctioneer's role in the contract.

How, if at all, has the auctioneer's role been changed by the Misrepresentation Act? Is he really only the intermediary agent between seller and buyer, with (as Mr Canaday put it) 'no responsibility whatsoever for attributions, authenticity, representations, faults, imperfections, inaccurate descriptions or anything else except the mechanics of the change of hands'? The position is obscure. The act makes no mention of auctioneers or, indeed, of agents. So if, as with Christie's in the case of Mr Spiro's 'Renoir', the auctioneers could claim legally to be only agents, then they can still do so. But if they can claim legally that they are not responsible for the way in which pictures are catalogued then the act becomes meaningless so far as art auction sales are concerned. For, if the auctioneer is not responsible for the attributions in his own catalogues then the vendors must be. But vendors generally are notoriously ill-informed about their own property as anyone working at the reception-counters of the great auction houses knows. Breaking the news to proud owners that their paintings, inherited from great-grandfather or Aunt Henrietta, are not, alas, what they have always thought they were, is a delicate task that staffs of the picture departments at Sotheby's, Christie's and Parke-Bernet must perform dozens of times every day.

In 1969 I had a personal experience that illustrates how the problem of authentication of works of art makes the Misrepresentation Act (*and* the much more comprehensive Trade Descriptions Act 1968) as applied to the art trade, about as useful as a sieve with a large hole in the middle. I had sent for sale at Sotheby's in December that year a watercolour drawing by Constantin Guys which I had bought at Agnew's about six months earlier for £405. It was listed and illustrated in the catalogue of a sale of 'Impressionist and Modern Draw-

84

ings and Watercolours' held on 11 December, but a few minutes before the sale I was told by an embarrassed member of Sotheby's staff that my lot had been withdrawn. The following day the auctioneers wrote to me that my picture

> was seen just prior to the sale by the greatest authority on Constantin Guys, Mr Bruno Streiff, who stated categorically that the watercolour had nothing to do with the hand of the artist. Since Mr Streiff is regarded as the foremost authority on Guys, and is also preparing the catalogue *raisonné* we had no alternative but to withdraw your watercolour from the sale.

In the catalogue of the sale the provenance had been given as 'Thos Agnew, London', a fact which later prompted a Sotheby man to remark that I was lucky to have bought it at Agnew's because they would be certain to take it back and refund the cost price without argument. But Agnew's did not see it that way. They replied that they did not agree with the opinion of Mr Streiff, of whom they had never heard (and of whom, I had to admit, I had never heard before this incident). The drawing had been bought in Paris from a perfectly respectable source, they said, and they 'were confident in the attribution to Guys'. In view of that, they added, they did not feel obliged to return the cost of the picture but offered to sell it for me and so recover my money.

This was a blow to me. Agnew's were, of course, entitled to contradict the opinion of Bruno Streiff and maintain that the drawing was, in their opinion, a genuine work by Constantin Guys. But with Sotheby's and Streiff against the drawing, I felt it was out of the question for me to sell it as a work of Guys or to allow Agnew's, or anyone else, to sell it as such *on my behalf.* The fact that, as Sotheby's put it 'a serious doubt, to say the least' had been cast upon the drawing, would, I believed, have made it an offence against the Misrepresentation Act for me to sell it as a Guys. But I was probably wrong, for the act (which was not, of course, framed primarily with works of art in mind), if applied to the case of the Constantin Guys drawing, becomes fatuous.

Whether or not the drawing is genuine or false, there can be no doubt that Agnew's could prove that they believed it to be genuine up to the time the contract was made. Therefore, they would not have been liable to return my money even if they had mistakenly attributed it to Guys. They were thus within their rights in refusing to take it back from me. But having taken it back (in fact they did so, but refunded only ninety per cent of the cost price) would they be legally entitled to sell it again as a work of Guys? The answer would appear to be 'Yes', since they could still claim 'reasonable ground' (based on their own expertise and the fact that the drawing had been in a famous collection) for believing that it was by that artist. But what would have been the position if *I* had kept the drawing and sold it as a 'Guys'? Could I have justified the sale by maintaining that, in spite of Sotheby's and Bruno Streiff, I preferred to accept Agnew's attribution and that was 'reasonable ground' for believing, up to the time I sold it, that the drawing was by Guys? Perhaps I could, but fortunately for me this fine legal point was not put to the test.

Attributions made in good faith, as distinct from deliberately false ones, are still only opinions, no matter who takes them. A friend of mine had a very striking experience of this inescapable truth. A painting by a modern German artist that he had bought in a London saleroom, was seen by a German expert of whom he had never heard) who said it was either 'wrong' or a very bad example of the artist's work. It was then shown to a British expert on the same artist who thought it was 'right' until told of the German expert's opinion, then he agreed with the German. Next it was taken to Sotheby's where a young man in the Impressionist and Modern department, who said he knew the picture, unhesitatingly valued it at 'six to eight hundred pounds'. Later it was seen by a London dealer who, knowing the various experts' various opinions nevertheless offered to consult yet another expert. This expert, who had once organised an important exhibition of the artist's work and written a learned monograph for the catalogue, bought the picture!

The art trade being the big business it is, the most powerful opinions are not necessarily those of the most scholarly experts. The most influential sources of attributions in Britain today are undoubtedly the great auction houses. But the very nature of their business requires that members of their staffs have a wide general knowledge of art rather than specialist knowledge of specific artists' work. Nevertheless, a rejection of a picture by Sotheby's or Christie's can damn a picture throughout the art trade. Only the more powerful, influential and esteemed dealers can afford to handle a picture that they have refused however strongly it may be felt that the auctioneers are wrong.

Yet if we look at the post-Misrepresentation Act catalogue of both houses we find that both are most anxious not to be thought infallible. Both, as we have seen, include comprehensively disclaimer clauses in their conditions of sale. Christie's, who seem to be almost paranoid about it, repeat the disclaimer at even greater length in a special 'Notice' in each catalogue. It is from this 'Notice' that the quotation that heads this chapter was taken.

6

Fakes, Fiddles, and Good Business

I see now how fruitless an interest is the history of art, and how worthless an undertaking is that of determining who painted, or carved, or built whatsoever it be. I see now how valueless all such matters are in the life of the spirit.

BERNARD BERENSON

Fakes never deceive by their devilish cleverness; one is deceived by a false art criticism that has dispensed with looking.

DANIEL WILDENSTEIN

A kind of university exists for the training of forgers. It is kept going by the stupidity of purchasers.

AUGUSTO JANDOLO (19th-century forger)

During one week in 1961 I saw a play about the Dutch forger Han van Meegeren, reviewed a new book about art forgeries, and wrote a short article* about an exhibition called *Forgeries*

*The Tatler, 22 February 1961.

and Deceptive Copies which was held at the British Museum. For
a reason I will explain later I repeat that article here:

Forgery, always a fascinating subject, seems now to be more
fascinating than ever to the layman. On the day that I went to
the exhibition the crowds round the showcases were so dense I
had to fight my way in to get a glimpse of the unicorn's horn
(lent by Sir Kenneth Clark) and the mummified mermaid, both
dating from the seventeenth century, or of the phoney flint-axes,
produced by 'Flint Jack' around 1860, and the falsified fossils
originally intended, by the students who made them, simply as
a joke on a professor.

The exhibition extends far beyond the field of the graphic
arts. The activities of forgers and copyists in the realms of
natural history, ethnography, manuscripts, music, postage
stamps and numismatics are all illustrated extensively. Antiquities are divided under the headings Greek and Roman,
Egyptian and Western Asiatic, Medieval and Later, and Orien-
tal. Fake antique furniture is a conspicuous absentee – but there
is a modern Chinese fake of an eighteenth-century English
clock, complete with a spurious, but cunningly unreadable,
maker's signature.

Among the pictures and sculptures are the echoes of some
fine scandals. A group of imitation Corots recalls the crack that
'of 3,000 pictures painted by Corot, 10,000 are now in
America.' An oil painting in the style of an old Dutch master
commemorates the sensational career of Van Meegeren.

No less intriguing than the Van Meegeren story is that of
Peter Thompson, a large selection of whose antiquarian and
topographical drawings are on show. Whereas the Dutchman
invented merely a new 'period' for Vermeer, Thompson invented an entirely new artist. He called his creation 'Captain
John Eyre' and gave him not only an *œuvre,* but also a complete
and complex life history and character.

Thompson, who lived and worked in London around the
middle of last century, was a carpenter and builder with some

small talent for drawing architectural subjects. In turning to faking of old drawings he seems to have been prompted by some idea of getting his own back on the government, at whose hands he claimed to have suffered 'a severe loss'.

That he was no fool is plain from the fact that he made 'Captain Eyre' an amateur artist, thereby explaining the weakness of his drawings which, since they purported to have been made in the first half of the seventeenth century were of historical rather than artistic interest.

He gave Captain Eyre a precise birth date, 6 October 1604, and a pedigree. He made him a descendant of a famous Lord Mayor of London and endowed him with a distinguished military record in the service of both the Royalists and the Parliamentarians.

His enthusiasm and ambition for the Captain were enormous and no doubt led to his ultimate undoing. The drawings were usually elaborately annotated. On one the 'artist' wrote a long reminder to himself 'in ye next week to do Master Shakespere's house in ye Clink Street'! At another time he drew an imaginary portrait of Ben Johnson, supposed to be 'copied from a wall portrait in Master Shakespere's house'.

Not content with selling the Captain's originals, Thompson launched a scheme for selling etched reproductions of them and produced a prospectus with a list of subscribers headed by the Prince Consort! Even today, 'Captain Eyres' are still submitted to the British Museum's Print Room as genuine.

Apart from the deliberate fakes, there are in the exhibition a large number of copies which, though made in the first place without the object of deception, were accepted as originals at some time or other. Ruskin's admiration for Turner resulted in his encouraging many good artists to make copies of the master's watercolours, to the confusion of collectors.

Looking at some of these copies hung beside the Turner originals we get some small idea of the problem with which the experts are faced when one master copies another even greater contemporary. As, for instance, when Andrea del Sarto copied Raphael, or Rembrandt's pupils copied him.

Recalled in a collection of fascinating newspaper cuttings and photographs is the case of the 'Leonardo' bust of Flora which nearly caused an international art incident between Germany and Britain before World War One. Though it has been shown conclusively to most experts that the wax bust is a nineteenth-century work, it is still in Berlin's Kaiser Friedrich Museum.

It was bought by the Museum's director, Wilhelm von Bode, in 1909, for £8,000, but no sooner was it put on show than its authenticity was challenged, first by an English art dealer and then by an artist who gloried in the name of Albert Dürer Lucas and who remembered helping his father to make the bust in 1846. It was made in imitation of Leonardo da Vinci but not as a forgery.

Despite the evidence to the contrary Von Bode maintained until his death five years later that he had bought a genuine Leonardo. By trying to save his face in this way he contributed to the popular idea that all art experts are idiots. But though this exhibition recalls many cases where experts have been taken in, it shows far more in which the forger's skill and cunning has been outmatched by the expert's knowledge.

Looking back on it I see that I adopted a reprehensible attitude to what Mr John Berger* has described as 'one of those crimes for which the cat should be brought back'. The too frequent use of the word 'fascinating' betrays an attitude towards the forger that makes him out to be a bit of a hero. It is the attitude of the general public who for some reason, or no reason at all, delight in seeing experts on any subject 'taken down a peg or two'. The idea has been encouraged by the authors of popular books on the subject who never tire of telling how this or that artist turned to forgery to 'get his own

*In the *Observer*, 8 July 1962

back' on the critics who failed to recognise the merits of his genuine pictures. This sort of defence has been claimed for Van Meegeren, Jean-Pierre Schecroun (of whom more later,) and many others. (The defence of Thompson on the grounds that he was getting his own back on the 'government' was even better, since everyone wants to get his own back on the 'government'.) In some cases it may be true. It is certainly true that many successful forgers have given themselves away because they could not resist the temptation to boast that they had bested the experts. However, it should not be forgotten that the great majority of forgers do not come into this category, they don't want glory, they are content with money.

How much forgery of works of art is going on today? It is, of course, impossible to say but it is certain that more art frauds were perpetrated in the decade 1960-70 than in any other decade. The faker is as much a part of the art game as the dealer or the art auctioneer is, and when their business is booming he sees that his is, too.

By the mid-1950s the problem had become so great in France that a special branch of the Sûreté was set up to deal with it. The mass production of fake Utrillos after that artist's death in 1955 provided the police, the artist's widow, and his dealer M Paul Pétridès with a constant headache, and no one with any sense will buy a post-World War One Utrillo nowadays without an unimpeachable provenance to go with it. As any tourist in Paris who has ever seen a Utrillo must know, imitators of the artist's inferior, later works abound there. At least one of these imitators, Madame Claude Latour, was good enough to fool Utrillo himself although she did not try to. She boasted that she could copy the style of almost any modern artist but she always signed her pictures with her own name.

This, however, was no deterrent to a young dealer with get-rich-quick ideas. He bought her 'Utrillos' for a few hundred francs, changed the signature on them and sold them as genuine Utrillos. At the dealer's trial in 1948 Utrillo confessed that he could not be sure that he had not produced some of the Latours exhibited in court. During the following decade Utrillo forgeries were virtually mass-produced. M Pétridès who in 1959 published a *catalogue raisonné* of Utrillo's complete *oeuvre,* also recorded over a thousand forgeries that had been brought to his notice.

Once I was at the home, near Manchester. of the artist, Laurence Stephen Lowry (whose work, incidentally, has many affinities with that of Utrillo, although his abstemious and ascetic way of living could not be less like the Frenchman's) when an acquaintance of his called with a 'Lowry' he had just bought for a hundred pounds. One glance at it showed it to be a fake. Although the style of the painting bore a superficial resemblance to Lowry's style the picture was signed simply with an 'L'. This was obviously done deliberately by the faker, who must have known that Lowry has always signed his work 'L S Lowry' or occasionally, and early in his career, 'L S L', as a 'let-out' to cover himself against accusations of forgery. The proud new owner of this thing had called to ask Lowry when he had painted it. As gently as possible he was told that he had been cheated but, like most people in such circumstances, he was very reluctant to believe this and to Lowry's astonishment he asked, 'Are you sure it isn't yours? Isn't there some expert I could take it to for an opinion?' I had never seen Lowry angry before, but the idea that some 'expert' could know more about his own work than he seemed preposterous and he showed it. Afterwards, when I reminded him that many artists, including

Picasso, Augustus John, and above all, Utrillo, had signed works by other men sincerely believing them to be their own, he laughed and felt sorry for the victim. 'Still, it was a bit silly of him to think anyone would give him a picture of mine that size for a hundred pounds nowadays, wasn't it?' And of course he was right.

Offering their wares too cheaply is the commonest mistake made by forgers and fakers and those who try to pass on their productions. This was, I believe, the initial error of judgement that led to the exposure, by London dealer Jacques O'Hana, of the young French forger, Jean-Pierre Schecroun. Before one of his accomplices called at the O'Hana Gallery in 1962, Schecroun had succeeded in getting away, to the tune of £25,000, with the forgery of about eighty drawings, water-colours, and gouaches purporting to be by Picasso and other modern masters. When Mr O'Hana was offered some of these things he asked for a certificate of authenticity and was given one which was, of course, itself a fake. Schecroun, a skilful artist who had once been a pupil of Fernand Léger, was so well versed in the styles of the artists he faked that he could, for example, produce a convincing brush and ink bullfight draw-ing 'by Picasso' in three minutes. Obviously the once popular image of the art-forger labouring for months to imitate the work of an Old Master was out of date. The breed, of which Van Meegeren was king, became redundant with the art boom of the fifties. But it is not only because many modern artists' works now sell for prices comparable with those of Old Masters that forgers now concentrate on producing fake Impressionist and Modern pictures. Nor is it because such pictures are 'easier to do'. It is simply that the forger knows (perhaps, ironically, as a result of reading about methods of detecting forgeries) that

95

it is always safer for him to copy or imitate works of the period in which he himself lives. It is impossible for one artist to adopt the mentality and the spirit of another who lived in a totally different age and inevitably something of his own time must enter into the fake. Salvador Dali made this point succinctly when he said that 'being a modern painter is the only thing, no matter what you do, that you cannot avoid being'.

David Stein, the young forger of Modern masters, who in 1966 in New York, where he dispensed his fakes from his own prosperous gallery on Park Avenue and made a million dollars, avowed that it was essential for him to get inside the soul and mind of the artist before he could forge a particular man's work. Before he settled in New York he had operated in European capitals, including London, making 'hit and run raids' as Schecroun had done. Staying in an hotel with his wife he would find out what was likely to sell locally and then produce the required fakes in his hotel room. He always chose men of our time many of whom were, to his ultimate regret, still living. And it was one of these, his favourite, Chagall, who brought about his downfall. The story was told in a reprehensible, but highly readable, article in the *Daily Telegraph Magazine** from which I quote

> 'If only I had stuck to dead men,' he [Stein] said sadly, shaking his broad head.
>
> In New York his own customers and other dealers were begging for Picassos, Chagalls, van Dongens and other works and in most cases wary buyers insisted on getting certificates of authentication. The best type of guarantee is a statement in the artist's own hand, written on the back of a photograph of the work in question. Stein found he could forge the handwriting and signatures of up to a dozen artists.

*19 April 1968

In the most frantic day of his career he sold to a New York dealer at one o'clock in the afternoon three Chagall watercolours that had not been painted when he arose at 6 a.m. In the space of seven hours Stein had aged the paper with tea, invented subjects, executed the works in quick succession, dashed to a framer for a while-you-wait job, zipped on to a photographer for photostats of the pictures, run back to the studio to forge certificates of authentication and kept his appointment with the dealer with a few minutes to spare. 'He was satisfied and gave me a cheque for $10,500,' Stein related.

The dealer might have been satisfied with the pictures but not with their price tags. Stein had fallen into a fairly obvious trap. He was selling attractive 'Chagalls', with papers of authentication, for well below the going market rate.

And at that very moment Chagall was himself in New York!

He had gone there to see his huge twin murals placed in the Metropolitan Opera House in Lincoln Centre. The dealer fixed an appointment with the old artist and took along his three Stein-Chagalls. Stein learned later that Chagall looked at them and spluttered, 'Diabolical!'

'He was furious' Stein recounted. 'He wanted to tear them up on the spot. But the matter had to go to the District Attorney and the DA stopped him from destroying the evidence.'

Evidently the powers-that-be of the *Daily Telegraph Magazine* did not share John Berger's fierce animosity towards forgers. Their reporter, Ian Ball, found the half-British, half-French Stein 'a thoroughly likeable rogue' and his pen-portrait of the criminal was as romantically colourful as the fake Chagall that Stein, who at the time was on bail, turned out for the benefit of the magazine's photographer. Later Stein was convicted but after serving a prison sentence he emerged to find that the publicity he had received had made him so famous that he could go back to painting imitations of the Modern Masters, inscribe them 'In the style of Chagall (Picasso, Matisse etc.)', sign them with his own name, and sell them for substantial sums.

But soon Stein's progress was to be eclipsed by the discovery in the fake-firmament of a far cleverer star, Elmyr de Hory, described (this time in the *Sunday Times Magazine**) as 'the great art forger of the century'. Said the Magazine.

> Since 1946, when he discovered he could dash off Picassos, de Hory has produced about 1,000 wonderful imitations to a value, if they were real, of about £20 million – Renoirs, Modiglianis, Derains, Dufys, Matisses, Vlamincks; many of them turned out in a few hours for pocket money. De Hory modestly calls his talent 'a private insurance policy'. His low selling prices, his statelessness and clandestine private life kept him undetected until, in the early 1960s, he was turned into a cottage industry, working from Ibiza. An Egyptian ex-dancer named Fernand Legros took him over and sold him internationally. Legros's grand slam as a dealer was the sale of forty-four assorted fakes to a Texas oilman named Algur Meadows for a knockdown price of something over a million dollars. By the time the imitations were offered for sale they had acquired customs seals, testimonials from previous owners, *expertises* from art authorities, notes from the artists – all of them forged.

De Hory's story was the subject of a book† by the notorious Clifford Irving (who himself faked material for a book about the multi-millionaire recluse, Howard Hughes) in which, once again, forgers emerge as a species of hero, their victims as greedy idiots who, more or less, deserve what they get. (The book, which was withdrawn shortly after publication, is prefaced with a twelfth-century quotation: *If fools did not go to market, cracked pots and false wares would not be sold*).

Unlike Stein and Schecroun, and most of today's as yet unexposed forgers, who, since such things began to command

*8th March 1970
†*Fake!*, Heinemann, 1970

high prices, have devoted their talents to modern drawings, watercolours, and gouaches, de Hory also made imitations of the oil paintings of Modern Masters. He did this, he has always claimed, only under pressure from his importunate 'promoter', Fernand Legros. He argued again and again that because oil paint takes many years to dry and because, during those years, the appearance of a painting changes considerably, it would be foolhardy for a forger to use the medium unless he was prepared to keep the finished picture for years before selling it.

In February 1967, just after millionaire Meadows had been told by a consortium of American art dealers that his collection of Impressionist and Post-Impressionist pictures included forty-four fakes, Fernand Legros put six de Hory imitations into a sale at the French Government auction house in Pontoise, near Paris. It was presumably, to be Legros's last fling before fleeing from the menacing Meadows. And it would probably have brought him more than £50,000 had an auction-room employee not decided that one of the pictures, an oil landscape purporting to be painted by Vlaminck in 1906, needed a little superficial cleaning. Starting with a few rubs on the sky this unnamed government employee soon found that the pale blue paint of the sky came off with the artificial 'time-stain' that had recently been applied by Legros' partner, Réal Lessard.

It was the end of the trio's partnership but, like Stein, de Hory was soon to turn his notoriety to his own advantage. During the previous twenty years (in which he had several times tried unsuccessfully to make a living by creating pictures that were entirely his own) he had produced hundreds of drawings, watercolours, gouaches, and oil paintings that had been accepted as the works of famous modern artists. The present whereabouts of a large number, possibly a majority, of these works is unknown. Many must still be in circulation, going the rounds of dealers, collector-investors, and auctioneers. In the summer of 1973, which he spent in visiting London, de Hory told ,friends that he had just seen one of his imitations on view in a West End saleroom. At the time, he had come to London for an exhibition of his newest works, all of them pictures in the manner of modern masters but signed with his own name. There were also several series of lithographs imitating the styles of Modigliani, Dufy, Van Dongen, Matisse, Léger, Cézanne, and Derain. Each lithograph was numbered and signed, in pencil, by de Hory. As 'de Horys' they were, I thought, expensive at something over £100 each. But if they get into the hands of unscrupulous people, who remove de Hory's signatures and replace them with forged signatures of the masters, they could certainly command much higher prices from ignorant collectors and cause a lot of problems in the salerooms.

In spite of the enormous amount of publicity given to his alleged part in the Meadows case, de Hory remained free until January 10, 1974, when Interpol arrested him in Ibiza and he was held in Palma jail. At the time of writing the exact charges against him are not known. It is worth noting, however, that for a long time he has maintained that he never forged anyone's signature. It is worth noting, too, that according to Clifford Irving a 'chief of Paris police' has said that, in order to convict de Hory, the prosecution would have to have witnesses who saw him paint the paintings, sign them with false signatures and hand them over to Legros and Lessard, and would also have to prove that de Hory knew they were going to be sold as genuine master-works.

It certainly seems that art forgery is an extremely difficult

*Ibid, p 222.

crime to pin on anybody. In the mid-1960s London was plagued with a swarm of spurious watercolours purporting to be by John Singer Sargent. All came from an acknowledged expert on Sargent – the artist's biographer – and many were sold through Christie's to several major London dealers, including Agnew, the Fine Art Society, and Newman. Others were bought by the Maas Gallery direct from the biographer, Charles Merrill Mount, a New York-born artist who lived in Dublin. Mr Mount maintained throughout that he was acting only as a selling agent for people he had met as a result of his biographical research. But after the disclosure that the pictures were fakes Mr Maas, who had dealt with Mount only by post, decided to confront his supplier. Accompanied by his lawyer he went to Dublin and there found Mount in an apartment crammed with pictures many of which, at first glance, he said, 'had striking similarities to the disputed Sargents, but these were by Mr Mount'. Maas and the other dealers recalled all the 'Sargents' they had sold and reimbursed their customers. But, as the *Sunday Times* 'Insight' column revealed:

> Mr Mount refused to disclose the source of the paintings he had found, authenticated and sold; as he lives in Dublin he cannot be challenged in an English Court by the unfortunate dealers concerned.*

In spite of the boom in forgeries that has, inevitably, accompanied the boom in art prices, and in spite of the fact that the art forger now specialises in modern pictures, the major problem for today's art expert is not deliberate forgery, whether of old or modern art. The bulk of his work is provided by those artists of all periods who, without any intention to

Sunday Times, 17 September 1967

defraud, copied, imitated or followed the styles of masters of their own time whom they admired or of whom they were pupils.

Often the problem is so great that the authorship of a great masterpiece becomes a question of, as the *New Yorker* used to put it, 'which expert d'ya follow?' S N Behrman* tells how Joseph Duveen tried to sell to Andrew Mellon a painting which he and many experts believed to be by Giorgione. Mellon was delighted with the picture but wanted to know what the 'infallible' Bernard Berenson's attribution would be. 'There isn't a doubt in the world that B B will say it's a Giorgione', Duveen assured him. But he was wrong. Berenson decided it was an early Titian, 'perhaps his earliest work, but only half out of the egg, the other half still in the Giorgione formula'. Mellon refused the picture. Duveen, bloody-minded but by no means bowed, found another millionaire to buy it and, to avenge himself, contrived that it should ultimately go to the National Gallery, Washington, which was given to the American people by Mellon and houses his collection. The picture, *The Adoration of the Shepherds,* is there now. It is attributed to Giorgione.

The picture is, of course the same picture whether it is ascribed to Giorgione or to Titian. Why then, you may ask, does it matter so much who painted it? Especially in this case where both artists are great masters? The answer is for the most part that old thing – money. There is among scholars, of course, a disinterested desire to get at the truth in such cases but what could it have mattered to Mellon? True, he already owned plenty of Titians but the *Adoration* was unlike anything he had and he professed to be enraptured by it. However,

*Duveen, by S N Behrman.

although he had to rely upon experts to do his aesthetics for him he could do his own mathematics and he knew that if the painting was by Titian then Duveen was asking several hundred thousand dollars too much. For Titian, the pupil of Giorgione, has not his master's virtue of great rarity. He lived to be ninety-nine and never stopped working. Giorgione died at thirty-three and the number of pictures that can be attributed to him with certainty is less than a dozen.

Now let us imagine that Berenson had pronounced the picture to be, not by Titian, but by Palma Vecchio (this did, in fact, happen to another 'Giorgione' when Sir Philip Hendy prepared a catalogue of another American millionaire's collection) who was influenced by Giorgione and was, like him, a pupil of Giovanni Bellini. This would have knocked another hundred thousand dollars off Mellon's estimate of the picture's value. Yet it would have been the same picture. And it would have been the same picture if finally the great B B who once said 'Never stick to a mistake', had announced that he had decided it was by none of these but was a copy of a lost Giorgione by an unknown artist of the sixteenth or seventeenth centuries. Then the picture would have been comparatively valueless. But it would still have been the same picture.

This may sound far-fetched but similar, if not quite such spectacular, things are happening all the time. In 1954 the London dealer, Leonard Koetser paid 6,000 guineas at Christie's for what most dealers must have thought was a copy of a *Madonna*, by the Bolognese master, Francesco Francia (c. 1450-1517), the original of which was in the National Gallery. But Koetser claimed that his picture was the original and the Gallery picture the copy. Under pressure from Koetser and others the Gallery's scientists went to work and had to admit that he was right. The picture (which, incidentally, had been 'declared genuine' by the near-infallible Bernard Berenson) proved to be a skilfully-executed, but now worthless, nineteenth-century forgery.

Before he died in 1972, the Munich art dealer, Martin Porkay was known to the German press as an 'art detective' for his efforts to expose fakes, forgeries, and wrongly attributed pictures wherever he found them. In 1937 he had shown that a £130,000 Masaccio *Madonna* in the National Gallery, Washington, was by a twentieth-century Viennese artist. Later as a self-styled expert on Rembrandt he exposed fakes in several major European galleries. In 1961 he published a booklet in which he attempted to prove that a Rembrandt, bought two years earlier for 225,000 Deutschmarks by the Kunsthalle, Bremen, from a famous dealer, was a 'school' picture. This he followed up with a denunciation of a self-portrait of Rembrandt for which the Staatsgalerie, Stuttgart, had paid 3.65 million Deutschmarks.

In 1962 the Press stirred up what the *Sunday Express* described as 'one of the stormiest controversies in the art world for years' over twin versions of Rubens's *Diana and her nymphs,* one of which belongs to Mr Paul Getty, who was said to have paid £200,000 for it shortly before. The second version had been bought by the Cleveland Museum of Art for 'more than £100,000' in 1958. The question was 'Which twin has the master touch?' Said the *Sunday Express:*

> Only one painting can be the original. The other is likely to be a studio copy with finishing touches added by the master, and worth only a small fraction of its price.
>
> Other famous artists frequently made several copies of their works. Could Rubens have painted both pictures? Unlikely, for

although he often did several versions of the same subject the paintings are much too meticulously similar for both to be from his brush.

The painting which is finally acclaimed as the original deserves to rank in importance beside Rubens's *Adoration of the Magi,* which fetched £275,000 at a London auction in 1959.

What an extraordinary statement that last paragraph is, but how well it crystallises the crazy illogic of the art game, a house of cards built on the, often infirm, shoulders of the experts. Here are two very fine paintings each believed by different experts to be by that busy mass-producer of pictures and diplomat, Sir Peter Paul Rubens. While they are in dispute each is worth a fortune. But if the dispute is ever resolved in favour of the one, the other will be comparatively worthless. Yet they will still, like Duveen's 'Giorgione', be the same pictures.

In the case of Rubens, more that that of any other artist, such a situation is ridiculous because in nearly all his large canvases he employed assistants some of whom like Van Dyck, who was his pupil, and Frans Snyders, who was his studio-manager, were masters in their own right, and it is impossible to say with certainty how much of any joint work is by *the* master. According to one American art historian Rubens was as bogus as Baconians believe Shakespeare to have been. Rubens, more businessman than artist according to this theory, continuously passed off the work of others, especially Snyders, as his own. Far-fetched as such a theory may be it is not entirely without basis in the light of the way in which Rubens's studio operated nor in the light of his own statements. Until the eighteenth-century the artist was regarded as a craftsman like any other craftsman who, when the demand for his work became too much for him, employed assistants to help him. Only the crankiest or most fastidious of patrons commissioning a successful painter would have thought of insisting that the master must carry out the entire commission himself. So, in 1618, we find Rubens replying to Sir Dudley Carleton, who wanted to acquire some of his paintings but insisted that they be all his own work, that certain pictures were not copies 'because they have been retouched so skilfully by my own hand that they can hardly be distinguished from the originals'. And of a particular picture he wrote, 'As this reproduction is not yet finished I am going to retouch it throughout myself. So it will pass for an original if necessary.' After Sir Dudley had rejected such things Rubens offered him the other pictures which, he said, were entirely his work except that *as was his custom* he had had the landscape backgrounds painted by a man who was very good at that particular job.

The chances of either the Getty picture or the Cleveland picture being *entirely* by Rubens would seem, then, to be very slender, but by examining them side by side experts could probably add considerably to their knowledge and perhaps agree on the extent to which the master's hand is evident in each. When so much money is at stake, however, owners of paintings are often understandably reluctant to get at the truth. But in fairness to Mr Getty it should be recalled that when, in 1964, he was told that a painting he bought for £40 at Sothebys in 1938 was probably a genuine Raphael worth £250,000 or more, he remarked, 'I really don't mind whether it is the original Raphael or not. I just know I like it.' Fortunately for the art game only the very rich can afford to take this attitude. It would never do for everyone to go around buying what he likes instead of what the experts and dealers tell him he ought to like. (Later it transpired that Mr Getty did care enough about the authenticity of the painting to spend many hours in the British Museum Library trying to prove that it was 'right'. He had no success, but in 1966 tests made on the picture in the laboratories of the Metropolitan Museum, New York, convinced the museum's experts that it was the painting of the Holy Family commissioned from Raphael by Pope Julius II in 1509 and known since the eighteenth century as the *Madonna di Loreto*. Today it is valued at more than £2 million.)

For anyone contemplating joining the fakes and forgeries department of the game it may be of interest to note that among the reasons given by experts for believing that Mr Getty's Rubens and Raphael are original works by these masters is the fact that each has been shown, by X-ray or infra-red radiation, to have undergone changes in design during the painting process. These *pentimenti,* as they are called, may suggest to the forger a way of giving his work an added semblance of authenticity but he must remember that if he does so he must also find a way of making them appear like the real thing when his pictures are submitted to X-ray, infra-red or ultra-violet radiation techniques. Ironically the best guides to the forger's art were, for a long time, those books devoted to methods of investigating paintings and uncovering fakes. Today science has outstripped the forger of Old Master paintings. The Milliprobe, invented by Dr Edward Hall can analyse the chemical elements in a painting and print the results on an electric typewriter in a matter of minutes. Thus elaborate forgeries are now hardly worth the candle and it may well be that Van Meegeren was the last of his kind.

Major forgeries, whether of the Old or Modern Masters, are not likely to concern the sensible newcomer to the art game. At the lower level of the game where he will be serving his apprenticeship his enemy is not the skilled forger but the opportunist faker and trickster whose presence is blatantly evident in all but the top auction rooms and on most of the art-stalls in antiques supermarkets, in the shops of nine out of ten of the thousands of quasi 'antique-dealers' who have come to the game since the boom starting booming, and in the rapidly proliferating stock-lists that are sent to me through the post by retired business or professional men who, having 'always been interested in art', turn themselves into art-dealers overnight. Far too many of the London salerooms and ninety-nine per cent of those auctioneers-cum-estate-agents all over the country who have jumped on the picture-sale gravy train in these fat years are so lacking in art expertise that they are, wittingly or unwittingly, at the mercy of petty crooks.

Today, more than ever before, it's the name that counts. But buying 'names', unless you are prepared and able to pay the market price for them, may easily prove a finger-burning business. Only a small minority of wrongly attributed pictures are deliberate fakes. A much larger part of them are copies or imitations made, in all innocence by the thousands of amateurs who amused themselves in that way before the days of mass entertainment, cinema, radio and television. By adding signatures to the better examples of these amateur efforts certain gentlemen, whose only artistic accomplishment is that they can write 'Corot' or 'Constable' etc, are making a comfortable little living out of the gullible without any of the laborious business of actually painting or drawing anything.

In recent years the trick has been brought more up to date and the names or initials of modern masters are associated with drawings and paintings that often have little resemblance to the works of those masters. The trap is intended to catch the large numbers of novice collectors and tyro dealers who now buy direct from the salerooms and are always hoping to make, and thinking they have made, a 'find'. It may be a petty kind of fraud but it is a particularly cunning one, for in the unlikely event of a victim trying to get redress he will almost certainly find he has no legal leg to stand on. He has only his own stupidity to blame. Here are a few examples of the sort of thing I have seen a thousand times in the smaller London salerooms (and sometimes in the bigger ones, too):

(a) A nude drawing signed with an 'M' in a circle.

(b) Another nude signed 'John'.

(c) A head of a woman signed 'HM'.

(d) A watercolour of a French lawyer signed 'hD'.

In each case the signature attempts to imitate that of a famous artist – the 'M' for Maillol, 'John' for Augustus John, the 'HM' for Matisse, and the 'hD' for Daumier – but the drawings, although competent, usually bear very little resemblance to the work of these artists. Nevertheless they are deliberately intended to deceive someone into thinking that they might perhaps be early works, or works of an unfamiliar period, by those artists.

But let us suppose that you or I have bought these drawings for an average of, say, fifty pounds each and then we find that none of them is what we thought or hoped. We complain to the auctioneers. They draw our attention to the clause in their conditions of sale that says they are not responsible for errors of description etc, and, in any case, they never said these drawings were by any of the artists we named (they were catalogued as French or English Schools of the nineteenth or twentieth centuries, or somesuch). We ask who put them into

109

the sale and are told that is a confidence they cannot possibly break without the seller's permission. Let us imagine, however, that we do track down the vendor (he is probably a small-time dealer) and put our questions to him. He looks at us pityingly and says, 'If I thought they were by the people you say, do you think I would be daft enough to put them into that sale? As far as I know the 'M' is for Morris, John is John Smith, HM is Harry Mudd, and hD is for hotdog'. And as a parting shot he adds, 'If you know anywhere you can buy a Matisse or a Daumier for fifty pounds, let me know!' And of course he is right; we have been fools. But we have learnt a lesson and we will write the lost money off to 'experience' while the confidence trickster – that is, I suppose, what he is – goes on finding new victims.

The only people who could do anything about this sort of thing are those auctioneers who are being used as distributing agents. But usually their attitude is that if people are fools they must take the consequences. After all, they say, the buyer himself is hoping to get something for nothing or, at least, for far below its real price. Because they themselves are too experienced to be caught by such elementary tricks, reputable members of the art trade take these petty frauds far too lightly even when they are perpetrated by some their own, less reputable, colleagues. I remember being shocked many years ago when, after watching an unsigned picture catalogued as nineteenth century French School knocked down in a London saleroom for an unexpectedly good price, a member of the auctioneer's picture staff remarked with a laugh. 'I bet that has a signature on it next time I see it.'

Recently a provincial dealer told me that an unsigned painting he had sold as 'Norwich School' was on show in the window of a London West End gallery with the bold, newly-added signature, 'J. Thors', in the bottom right corner. I checked this and then asked him if he was sure that it had been unsigned. In corroboration he referred me to the restorer who had cleaned and relined the picture for him. The restorer, too, was sure there had been no signature. In this case the dealer would probably have argued that the painting was undoubtedly by the artist whose name it bore and that he would never attach a signature to any picture unless he was sure it was the right one. He would probably have argued, too, that his clients insisted on signed works and that it was, therefore, their fault if he had to do a little bit of jiggery-pokery to please them. There are collectors who, without any ability to recognise any particular artist's work, foolishly put far too much faith in a signature. Even the artist's name written on a drawing, without any attempt at forging his signature, will satisfy many buyers, especially if the drawing is old and the name is written in an old-fashioned hand. I know one collector of drawings who will have nothing but signed works and so his collection includes several 'signed' drawings by artists who are known never to have signed their work. The fact that a spurious signature will throw suspicion on a genuine drawing does not seem to have occurred to him. So long as such collectors exist there will be unscrupulous dealers who will satisfy their demands. A signature is superfluous to an unimpeachable drawing and it can add nothing to a drawing that is not 'right'. The aim of the collector must be to learn to recognise artists' styles, not just their signatures.

In his biography of Lucien Pissarro,* W S Meadmore tells a classic story about signature-faking and shows, at the same time,

*Lucien Pissarro by W S Meadmore.

how inadequate the law is to counter it. In the years just before the last war Lucien Pissarro, artist son of the great Impressionist master, Camille Pissarro, was preparing the complete catalogue of his father's works, when a friend reported that he had seen a Camille Pissarro in a small-time dealer's shop window. Lucien went to see the picture and recognised it as one of his own landscapes which had been sold at Sothebys in December 1936 for £22. But now his own signature had been removed and replaced with an imitation of his father's 'C Pissarro'. After establishing that the shopkeeper was in fact the man who had bought the picture at Sothebys he took legal advice and was told, to his dismay, that 'forgery of this description was not considered a criminal action under English law'. He could try bringing an action for damages but it would be difficult, said his solicitors, to convince a court that having one of his paintings passed off as the work of a great master had been damaging to his reputation!

Lucien persisted and made an application at Bow Street for a prosecution on the grounds of false pretences, but by this time the picture had been sold (for £450 to a buyer who could not be traced) and the magistrate ruled that unless the picture could be produced no case could be brought. Still Lucien fought on and eventually the case came up at the Old Bailey but was again dismissed. 'Now there is, of course, no doubt,' Lucien Pissarro wrote afterwards, 'that the case was tried perfectly fairly, and that the result was in accordance with the law. May one not suspect, however, that if a grocer had offered for sale margarine as fresh butter the result would have been different?'

One law for grocers and another for art-dealers? The dealer in this case certainly seems to have made his own law. His shop was filled with fakes to which he added appropriate signatures.

Jasper Johns's *Painted Bronze 1960* - one of two casts made from a couple of beer cans and then painted - fetched £37,037 ($90,000) when sold at Sotheby-Parke Bernet, New York, in October 1973. Alongside a photograph of this work in her book *American Painting since 1900**, art critic Barbara Rose says Johns 'has explored his themes with a kind of dogged logic, combining motifs, paraphrasing them, and changing their context, as if to extract the last drop of meaning from the most banal object'.

David Stein at Work on an imitation Chagall *(see Chapter 5)*

*Thames & Hudson, London, 1967

3   This drawing, *Lorette,* was sold to me in June 1969 by Agnew's as a work of Constantin Guys. But in December that year, when it came up for sale at Sotheby's, it was withdrawn at the last minute. Bruno Streiff, expert on Guys and author of the *catalogue raisonné* of the artist's work, had pronounced it 'wrong'. Agnew's disagreed, bought the drawing back and returned it to stock.

4   'Pablo Picasso *Tête de Jeune Fille Signed and dated 19.8.52, Brush and grey wash*' – so read the entry alongside this illustration in the catalogue of Christie's 'Impressionist and Modern' sale on May 2 1969. But the work was withdrawn before the sale. At about the same time an illustration of the same work appeared in the American edition of Clifford Irving's book *Fake* with the caption, 'Picasso: *Femme.* Painted by Elmyr [de Hory] in 1964'

This superb bronze statuette of a rearing horse (9 ins high) was bought in a 'job lot' at Christie's by Mr. Pierre Jeannerat way back in 1933. It was one of four bronzes that cost him 11½ guineas. From the start art-critic Jeannerat believed that it was a study for Leonardo da Vinci's *Trivulzio Monument* and over the years more and more experts have come to agree with his attribution to Leonardo, so that if sold at auction today it would probably make a record price for any sculpture.

This weird and wonderful painting, *The Temptation of Eve* by the 16th century German master Hans Baldung Grien, belonged to an Edinburgh school teacher, who had lived with it all her life and believed it to be worth a hundred pounds or two. To raise the money for the deposit on a new car she took the picture to Sotheby's. It fetched £224,000.

7 This large, fine, unmistakable
Gainsborough masterpiece, was
taken to Sotheby's by two sisters who
had known the picture all their lives
but believed it to be a copy. Called
(incorrectly, it is said) *Mr and Mrs
John Gravenor and their daughters
Elizabeth and Dorothea*, it was
completely unrecorded and unknown
to scholars and dealers but it sold for
£280,000.

Mother and Child by the German Expressionist painter Christian Rohlfs, bought by the author in 1968 for £1 at a London sale, in which it was catalogued simply as 'Modern School'. It measures 40 ins by 25 ins, is signed with the artist's initials and dated '18. Today it would fetch several thousand pounds.

The massive (7ft x 10ft) masterpiece *Daniel in the Lions' Den* by Rubens *below* was bought by art dealer Julius Weitzner for £500 at Bonham's, the London auction house, a week before the sale in August 1963 in which it was scheduled to be offered. From an illustration in the sale catalogue, where it was listed as a joint-work of Jordaens and De Vos, it was immediately recognised by several dealers as a famous Rubens. But by that time the picture was already on its way to America where it was later acquired by the National Gallery, Washington, for more than £170,000.

10 *L'Etudiant à la Chasse*, a painting from the collection of American multi-millionaire René Fribourg, was sold by Sotheby's as a work of Alfred de Dreux in June 1963. It fetched £400. Three years later, again at Sotheby's, it was knocked down to me for £50. Hopefully I put it into Bonham's saleroom where, with its excellent provenance (which now included Sotheby's) it was expected to fetch £500 or more. In fact it made £80.

11 This large canvas, *St. Sebastian*, was bought for 'a few pounds' by art dealer Julius Weitzner from an Essex pickle factory where it had hung unprized for years. It was authenticated by the country's top Rubens-expert, Michael Jaffé, as an unfinished composition by the Flemish master. But when, in 1970, it came up for sale at Sotheby's it was bought in at only £800!

A case of Wishful Thinking (see
Chapter 8)

Above: Terracotta figure of *Day*, once
attributed to Michelangelo, but now
believed to be by the great master's
pupil Tribolo.
    Museum of Fine Arts, Houston,
                                Texas.

Right: Plaster cast, presumably made
from the terracotta. Note the lines
indicating the joins of the
piece-mould in which it was cast.
    Photograph published 1876, Leipzig

Bottom: A 19th Century bronze
evidently made from the plaster cast,
obviously with some loss of definition
and power further compounded by
19th Century-style finishing.
    Colln. E. Halprin, Richmond, B.C.

13   *An Auction is a publick Sale,*
      That injures those who fairly deal –

So reads the caption to this 18th Century engraving. But today the worst enemy of those who go to auctions with ideas of fair dealing are buyers with vastly more money than sense. In the week beginning with April Fool's Day 1974, Sotheby's and Christie's between them sold more than £6 million of Impressionist, Modern and Contemporary works of art. Never before were the effects of uncontrolled international inflation and the consequent 'flight from money' by the rich more blatantly evident. The following plates illustrate some of the things they bought.

14 **Quality Before Quantity —**
This mini-masterpiece *Jockeys avant
le Départ* by Degas, ($3\frac{3}{4}$ ins by $4\frac{3}{4}$ ins)
fetched £68,000, nearly £4,000 a
square inch, at Sotheby's on April 2,
1974. It was in the sale of a
collection formed, between 1895 and
1930, by 90-year-old Argentinian
Antonio Santa Marino and was a gift
to him from the dealer Georges
Bernheim, from whom he had bought
several pictures, including Daumier's
*Avant l'Audience – L'Avocat et son
Client.* This drawing in pencil,
watercolour and gouache, only 7 ins
by $8\frac{1}{2}$ ins, realised £60,000.

15 **Quantity Before Quality? —**
Don't worry about the quality, look at the quantity you could get for your money at Sotheby's Contemporary Sale on April 3 and 4, 1974.

Cy Twombly's $6\frac{1}{2}$ ft by 8 ft *Bolsena*, oil and pencil on canvas, cost only £21,000 – cheap if you think of it as less than £3 a square inch.

Tom Wesselman's *Great American Nude No. 73* – 6 ft by $7\frac{1}{4}$ ft of it – was similarly cheap at £17,500. Painted in 1965, it first belonged to Belgian industrialist Philippe Dotremont (see Chapter 4) who collected modern American paintings because they had the freshness of spring. Presumably the bloom had faded on this one.

16 **Oddity Before Quality Or Quantity?**
For the progressive collector tired of
old fashioned paintings on canvas,
the sale at Sotheby's on April 3/4,
1974, offered a variety of
contemporary *objets d'art* ranging in
price from a modest £920 for an
Andy Warhol *Campbell's Tomato
Juice Carton above* (an empty
wooden box with silk-screen printed
lettering) to £12,100 for a *Package
overleaf top* made of canvas, rope
and string by Bulgarian Christo
Javacheff in 1963. Since he made
this 'work' Christo the Wrapper has
gone on to ever greater things
packaging nude girls, haystacks,
buildings (including the whole of the
Museum of Contemporary Arts,
Chicago) and – his biggest project to
date – a mile of rocky Australian
coastline which involved a million
square feet of fabric, 35 miles of rope
and £54,000. Nicely placed pricewise
between Warhol's *Carton* and
Christo's *Package* was Claes
Oldenburg's *Two Hats, overleaf*

bottom described as 'muslin baked in
plaster over wire frame, painted with
enamel, signed with initials and dated
1961'. When it was exhibited in New
York that year the artist priced it at
249 dollars and 99 cents. At
Sotheby's thirteen years later it cost
£8,500.

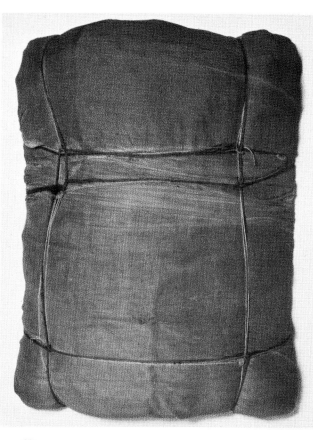

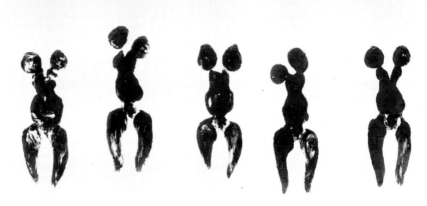

17 The illustration *top* from the Tate
Gallery's catalogue for its Yves Klein
exhibition in 1974 shows how the
artist created what he called his
Anthropométries. Before an invited
audience he directs three nude
models, who smear their bodies with
paint and press themselves against a
large sheet of paper. On this
occasion the demonstration was
accompanied by twenty musicians
playing Klein's own *Symphonie
Monoton* – forty minutes of 'one
single, continuous, long-drawn out
sound'. (See Chapter 11)
Above: One of the more successful
products of the procedure,
*Anthropometry of the Blue Period,
1960,* which was shown at the Tate.

Concurrently with the Klein exhibition
the Tate showed works by Piero
Manzoni *overleaf,* most of them white
reliefs made of mundane things like

bed-linen, cotton-wool, painted
bread-rolls. But Manzoni also made
objects intended to satirise the
commercialism of art and which,
ironically, are now highly valued in
the world of art commerce. These
included balloons that were filled with
the artist's breath and tins filled with
his excrement. Single lines on rolls of
paper in sealed containers, wrapped
boxes containing air, parcels made of
canvas – all ceased to be works of
art only if they were opened. He
signed people and made them into
sculptures and transformed objects
into works of art by placing them on
a magic pedestal. He turned a large
pedestal upside down on the ground
and so made the whole Earth a
sculpture. He held an exhibition of
scores of hard-boiled eggs signed
with his thumb-print and all were
eaten by visitors in seventy minutes.

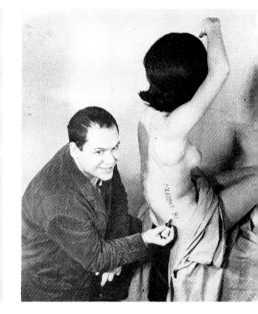

18 *Equivalent*, an arrangement of 120
    bricks by American artist Carl Andre,
    was among a number of
    'masterpieces of minimal art' on show
    at the Tate Gallery from January to
    April 1974.

19 *Felt Piece* by Robert Morris was one
    of the American contributions to the
    exhibition *When Attitudes Become
    Form* at the Institute of Contemporary
    Arts, London, in 1969. To the right of
    the photograph is a British
    contribution, Barry Flanagan's *Rope
    Sculpture*, a length of 6 ins-diameter
    rope straggling across the gallery
    floor. When shown in New York a
    similar 'rope sculpture' by Flanagan
    was claimed to provide 'an
    introduction to the experience of
    space and the inflections of shape
    through its infinite possibilities and
    delineations'.

Pop Art was already as good as dead in December 1970 when the shortlived Mayfair Gallery, London, held an exhibition called *Pop! '70,* but in a banal attempt to enliven the show one live item was introduced – a girl's breast. On view only on Saturdays from 10 till 6, it was part of American artist Tom Wesselmann's *Bedroom Titbox,* which was described as a work in 'oil, acrylic, collage and live tit'. The appendage belonged to an artist's model who was paid to lie, uncomfortably concealed, on a hastily constructed shelf above the glazed box in which was arranged an artificial still-life.

If a customer brought a picture back he said that he had sold it in good faith and immediately gave the customer his money back.

I was particularly interested to read in Mr Meadmore's account that some of these fakes were produced by an artist in Manchester at thirty shillings each. In 1964, when I went with L S Lowry to Manchester to visit a number of private collectors, I heard repeatedly of a dealer, in business there until he died a few years earlier, who could always satisfy collectors' requirements with suspicious promptitude. No matter what a customer yearned for the dealer always knew where he could get hold of one. A Constable? A Sickert? A Manet? – someone he knew had the very thing. It would take only a few days to get it. From what I saw it appeared that the dealer kept a sizeable stock of fairly good quality paintings and drawings by unknown artists and from this he chose one that had some (often very slight) stylistic resemblance to the work of the master his client admired. All he needed then was a few days' drying-time for the signature he would add to the picture (drawings did not take so long to procure!).

Nowadays, when the majority of people who are buying pictures know nothing and care less about art, the importance of signatures has become absurdly overrated. As a result, such people are not only easily deceived by spurious signatures; they are also willing to pay far too high prices for genuine ones. In no sector of the game is this more apparent than in that crazy half-art-world where mechanical reproductions of paintings, signed by the artist are erroneously described as 'artist's proofs'* and sold in editions of several hundreds at prices up to

*Artist's proofs are impressions of an original print (ie an etching, lithograph, woodcut, wood engraving etc) which the artist takes for himself *before* producing

113

£150 for each reproduction.

In a curious article (it read like an advertisement), which appeared in the *Daily Telegraph* in November 1973, these signed reproductions were said to 'rank nowadays with property, vintage wines and Rolls Royce "Corniche" motor-cars as the profitable investments', and a lot of figures were quoted to show that a lot of people were making a lot of money out of them. The author of the article, one Sam Heppner, also informed his readers that the number of reproductions in any one edition is limited by the Fine Art Trade Guild to a maximum of 850. Even so, a little simple arithmetic – 850 × £150, or even 850 × £50 – shows that the 'artist's proof' business is very big business. Yet what do you get if you buy one of these things? You get a colour reproduction (usually produced by either the commonplace half-tone process or by photolithography) which is worth two or three pounds (you can buy similar things for that little at the Tate Gallery or from commercial publishers such as the Medici Society, Soho Prints, or Athena) *plus* the autograph of an artist which, according to his or her importance, is worth between 25p and £2 in the autographs market. The profits are enormous and, as Mr Heppner pointed out, that is only the beginning. Every time these reproductions change hands in the idiot-fringe market the price goes up by fifty per cent. Good short-term investments they have certainly been, but when sanity returns to the art market they are surely going to be virtually valueless, the junk of the not-so-distant future.

those that are to be published and/or sold. They are usually signed by the artist and marked 'ap' (artist's proof) or 'ea' *(épreuve d'artiste)*. Apart from the fact that they are signed, they have nothing whatsoever in common with those mechanical reproductions of pictures by such artists as Lowry, Bradley, Dawson, Shepherd, which are currently being purveyed as 'artist's proofs'.

So far in this chapter I have discussed only ways in which you may be cheated or may cheat yourself when you are buying a picture. But you may also be cheated when you are selling a picture. And even while you are sitting at home without the slightest thought of selling a picture it is possible that there is a 'knocker' not far away plotting to separate you from your family heirloom for a little of its true value. Perhaps tomorrow morning he will knock on your door, hand you his card, and say, 'Good morning, madam' – he rarely calls when husbands are at home – 'forgive me for troubling you' – he is very polite – 'I have an urgent order from America for pieces of Victoriana – glass, furniture, pictures, and so on. It doesn't matter about the condition as long as it is the right age. We will take almost any old thing you want to get rid of and we pay the best prices. You haven't anything? You would be surprised, madam. If you just let me have a quick look round I can give you an idea of the sort of thing I have in mind. Why, even that old umbrella-stand there could be worth ten pounds to you'.

This is where you should say, 'No, thank you' and shut the door. But ten pounds for that horrible old umbrella stand!* Heavens, he might take that terrible old brass fender and fire-irons that you haven't used since the central heating was put in. You are sunk, he is inside now and his eyes are whizzing round the place pricing everything like an electronic cash-register. Funny thing, he doesn't seem to look at all the things you thought were rather good. At this stage he may ask to see upstairs (or, if he has brought an accomplice along – they often hunt in pairs – the accomplice may ask where the 'loo' is and have a quick snoop round while looking for it). Up there

*At Christie's in 1972 an 'umbrella-stand' that turned out to be a fourteenth-century Chinese wine jar, fetched £220,500.

115

he goes through the same calculating motions. He admires some of your furniture (it's reproduction) but regrets that it is the 'wrong period'. You show him the brass fender in the junk room and you are just about to beg him to take it away for nothing when he says, 'Can't offer you more than five pounds for it. Not much demand for them nowadays'. You are delighted. He rummages around the junk while you assure him there is nothing else there. On his way out of the room he notices, apparently for the first time, that old picture in the huge gilt frame that you threw out of the drawing-room when you redecorated last year. 'Would you like to sell that frame?' he asks. It's a terrible, dull, heavy Victorian gilt thing, so you say 'yes'. 'Just the sort of thing they like in America', he says. 'Give you a fiver for that, too.' He picks it up to take downstairs. 'Don't forget the fender,' you say and he laughs and picks that up too.

At the front door he takes out his bulging wallet and hands you two fivers. He has forgotten about the umbrella-stand and you don't like to ask him about that but you say timidly, 'I thought you only wanted the frame not the picture'. Maybe he will give you a couple more pounds, you think. Instead, he laughs and says. 'Oh I'm sorry. Of course I don't want the picture.' And he begins to fumble with the back to get it out of the frame. When he asks you for a hammer and pliers you probably say, 'Oh don't bother,' and let him keep the picture. If you bring him the hammer and pliers he will probably say, 'Oh, it doesn't matter. I won't take the frame,' and put out his hand for you to return one of the fivers. Or he may offer you a few pounds for the picture which is, he says, 'just a print', or 'an amateurish copy'. He may, of course, be right. Unless your husband comes home and says, 'My God! That was the family

Turner you've given away!' you will probably never know. Only one thing is certain – the knocker did not pay you more than it was worth. He is going to make a profit, perhaps only 100 per cent, perhaps 100,000 per cent.

This is an old-fashioned technique. Modern knockers have many much cleverer methods, the most diabolical of which was exposed by a team of *Sunday Times* reporters who had investigated what the paper called 'the antiques game'. Following up a newspaper advertisement in which a self-styled 'internationally known art expert' (formerly a secondhand-car dealer) offered to value, attribute, restore or buy fine oil paintings and sporting prints, they interviewed two women who had been visited by the advertiser. The first told how the 'art expert' tried to trick her and browbeat her into parting with two paintings (afterwards valued by Christie's at £200 each) for £40. The second, the widow of a diplomat, showed him a set of four sporting pictures by Reinagle, which she believed were valuable, and at his request, allowed him to take them away for 'expert examination by his colleagues'. In fact, he took them to Christie's and was told that they would fetch over £4,000 at auction. He then returned to the owner with the bad news that the paintings were in poor condition and that the market was against a quick sale. In spite of that he was prepared to take a gamble and give her, say, £400 for them. She accepted, and he took the pictures straight to Christie's where they were sold for £4,725.

This was a case of deliberate fraud. Most knockers would not go so far. Like the members of the rings they argue that their successes are made possible only by the stupidity of the public, but unlike the ring-men they do not consistently break the law. Generally you will never know what happens to the picture you sell to a knocker for, say, five pounds. But if you learn that he has sold it for a thousand and challenge him, he can always answer that, at the time, he thought he was giving you a fair price. And even now, when the Misrepresentation Act and Trade Descriptions Act are supposed to protect you, there is probably (as we saw in the last chapter) nothing you can do about that.

Having heard many true stories like that, I always treat with suspicion newspaper advertisements about pictures wanted, even though it must be foolish to think every advertisement of this kind is a trap. There must sometimes be good reasons why genuine buyers use this method of doing business (although I can't think of one that would be in your favour). All I am advocating is caution, especially when the advertisement begins 'Private Collector wishes to buy . . .', which almost invariably means that the advertiser is some sort of dealer, or when one ends 'No Dealers', which means 'no one with any knowledge wanted'.

When you are buying don't be afraid to ask for assurances of authenticity – a good dealer will always guarantee to take a picture back if you prove his description of it to be false. And when you are selling, be sure you know what it is you are selling and try to get some idea of its market value before you approach a buyer. This is important even where you are selling to a reputable dealer. And it is doubly important if you are selling at auction, unless you go to the top. Even there, don't believe everything you are told. Both Sotheby's and Christie's are inclined to err on the low side when giving estimates and suggesting reserve prices. The reasons are obvious. They don't want your picture to be 'bought in' and they know that you will feel happier if your picture sells for substantially more than

118

your low reserve than you will if it just reaches a higher reserve. That's auctioneer's psychology.

7

It's a Knockout

An auction is a publick sale,
That injures those who fairly deal.
Verse from an eighteenth-century print

Many years ago I attended a country sale of pictures which turned out to be an almost complete compendium of the booby-traps which may be laid, consciously or unconsciously, for the unwary. The catalogue listed works by almost every distinguished water-colourist from Paul Sandby to Wilson Steer, included the inevitable 'Corot', and concluded with a few things by such artists as Munnings and John. It was obviously too good to be true and it meant a journey of two hundred miles, but once you have the saleroom-bug you don't let little things like those deter you. I went.

Before the sale began there were two hours for viewing but it took only a minute to see that it was a very curious sale. About sixty per cent of the property was junk, about thirty-five per cent the sort of odds and ends that sell for a few pounds in the smaller London salerooms, and about five per cent was made up of drawings and paintings of some quality. A large proportion of the drawings and watercolours had, apparently, been newly mounted and framed for the sale, and a surprisingly large number of the other pictures bore the marks of a London auction-room on their backs. From these two facts I drew the conclusions that those things in the first category had been put into the sale by a dealer and that most of those in the second had been considered but not accepted for sale in London. In both cases the signs read 'proceed with caution', for dealers do not usually sell works by 'big names' in the country unless they have first tried to get them sold in London, and London salerooms do not turn down 'big name' pictures, unless they are, to put it mildly, doubtful about them.

Again there was an unusually high proportion of mounts and frames bearing the names of famous artists – Peter de Wint, Paul Sandby, Francis Towne, John Sell Cotman, Myles Birket Foster, and so on. All were competent and many were charming old watercolours and drawings, but the 'De Wint' was not a De Wint, the 'Sandby' was not a Sandby, the 'Towne' was not a Towne, the 'Cotman' was not a Cotman, and the 'Myles Birket Foster' was not a Myles Birket Foster in spite of its bearing a monogram that looked very like his. And needless to say the two 'Corots' were nothing like Corots although they were in frames labelled 'J B Corot'. A drawing signed 'John' may have been by John somebody-or-other but it was certainly not, as the catalogue claimed, by Augustus John. Yet a horsey thing by Munnings was unmistakably 'right' and, even more unexpected in this sort of company, there was a small seventeenth-century Dutch interior of first-class quality. It was catalogued baldly as 'an old picture of peasants in an inn'.

It was this last painting that attracted most attention and I noticed many men whom I took to be dealers or dealers' runners examining it closely. But when the sale began none of these dealers was present. The auctioneer was agonisingly slow. After an hour he had sold only forty out of the two hundred lots (at Sotheby's and Christie's the rate is at least twice as high and in some of the other London salerooms they move three times as fast).

I left the room for a 'breather'. In the pub next door six or seven of the missing dealers were sitting talking. I stood at the bar with a drink and listened. They were discussing what they could do about a gentleman named Weston who had refused repeatedly to join them. I realised that I was in the presence of 'The Ring'. When I turned to look at them the man who was evidently their leader put a finger to his lips and silenced them.

When I returned to the saleroom the auctioneer was nearing Lot 100 but there was still another hour to go before the best things would be sold. A few minutes before the hour was up the seven dealers came in and stood near the door. Another few minutes more and they moved into the body of the room and one of them separated from the others and took up a position where he could be easily seen by the auctioneer – and by his fellow dealers. The Dutch picture came up and the auctioneer asked for 'ten pounds to start'. The lone dealer nodded. The price went fairly quickly to forty pounds and stopped. Instead of coaxing his audience for more bids as he had done *ad nauseam* throughout the sale the auctioneer seemed anxious to knock the picture down quickly. 'All done at forty pounds then', he said and raised his hammer. I waved my catalogue at him. I had had no intention of bidding because I estimated that the picture would fetch at least two hundred and fifty pounds, but now I made up my mind to bid up to one hundred. I did not expect to get it for that but the indecent haste with which the auctioneer wanted to knock it down to the ring needled me into determination that they should pay a reasonable price for it. I went on bidding to a hundred – and beyond. Suddenly, at one hundred and ten pounds, the ring's man shook his head. 'Yours sir,' the auctioneer said bringing down his hammer with a harder-than-usual bang. 'May I have your name please'. Unexpectedly I was the owner of 'an old picture of peasants in an inn'. It turned out to be, as I had at first guessed and later hoped, a work of David Teniers the Younger.

This was my first first-hand experience of a ring at work. Several times since, I have made very good buys by outbidding petty rings in smaller salerooms and at private-house sales. The whole *raison d'être* of a ring is (as we shall see) such that if you succeed in outbidding them for something you want you will probably get a bargain. But to make a habit of it with the same ring members is not to be recommended. Unless your knowledge is superior to their collective knowledge you may find you are being deliberately 'taken for a ride' and made to pay far too much. I often wonder what my first ring did to poor Mr Weston. I doubt if they were content simply to damage the things he bought before he could take possession of them, which is one of the charming ways they might use for getting their own back on those who dare outbid them.

The basic principle of 'the ring' is simple. It is to divert from the owner to themselves as much as possible of the true value of an item sold at auction. But the way in which a ring operates may be far from simple. Understandably those dealers who take part in rings are reluctant to reveal to outsiders how they work, but in November 1968 an anonymous antique-dealer, who clearly knew all the answers, 'blew the gaff' in the *Observer*. At the time auction rings were the subject of a great deal of comment in the Press and questions in Parliament following an announcement that the National Gallery had paid £150,000 for a small painting by Duccio (active 1278-died 1319), which had been bought seven months earlier for £2,700 at a country-house sale. The implication was that a ring had been operating at the sale and that the man who had bought the picture and sold it to the National Gallery, the well-known London-based American dealer, Julius Weitzner (of whom more in the next chapter), had been involved with the ring. The President of the Board of Trade (Mr Crosland), after being pressed to have the matter investigated, complained of meeting a wall of silence in his enquiries and of not being given essential evidence until it was too late to bring a prosecution. Throughout, Mr Weitzner steadfastly denied that he was at the head of a dealer's ring, and claimed, 'This whole thing has been sparked off by jealousy because I have made a great many discoveries of works of art.'

In this country things of this sort always seem to be allowed to fade away, and this was no exception. But two good things came out of it. The first was the *Observer* article, which the paper quite rightly claimed as 'the most detailed account yet published' of how a ring works. The second was an hilarious column which the affair prompted Bernard Levin to write for the *Daily Mail*. For posterity I reproduce them both here:

HOW THE ART RING BOYS STAGE A KNOCKOUT*
Actually, the word 'Ring' is rather *démodé*. It signals to a member that the speaker is not one of 'the Boys'. The in-word is 'KO', meaning knockout, but 'the 'Knockout' and 'the Settlement' are also frequently used.

Observer, 24 November 1968

The aim of the Ring is quite simple. A group of dealers agree privately not to bid against one another during a public auction, and to share out privately among themselves afterwards the lots they have bought. This gives them two advantages. First, by eliminating powerful competition, they keep saleroom prices down. Secondly, when they auction the lots privately afterwards, the difference between the artificially low saleroom price and the more realistic price at the Knockout is shared between the members of the Ring.

Membership is flexible. The Settlement operates at every sale in Britain where it is profitable for a chosen few to 'stand in'. Every region has its local Settlement, and the Boys may participate in those adjacent areas without too much trouble.

Admission to membership is governed by an indeterminate consensus of the old guard, at first always on a temporary or probationary basis. The qualifications for a candidate are knowledge, financial power, courageous bidding and verbal discretion – in short, his known sustained nuisance value in relation to the Knock.

Members who recognise a dangerous opponent will discuss with one another and with their chairman whether he should be 'taken in'. If this is agreed, one of them will be delegated to suggest to the candidate: 'Leave it alone, you'll be all right today'.

Usually, the temporary member does not settle with the Ring itself, but with the member representing it – in a sort of ante-Ring. He is asked which of the lots he wants of those bought by the Ring. These are 'knocked out', that is, they are bid for at once between himself and the representative.

In the unlikely event of his successfully 'claiming' any of these (that is, outbidding the representative), he will in each case pay the sum he has bid plus the original price paid at the sale.

At the end, he will receive in return the lots he has claimed plus a share of the total amount bid by the two of them in their mini-settlement (e g if there are eight members of the Ring proper, he will receive a ninth part of this sum, the rest going into the pool for the boys to share later). He is then dismissed, and plays no further part in the KO.

But the Ring now knows precisely what his strength is as an opponent. He will always be 'called out' in this way at future sales unless he is eventually expelled from the Settlement for not claiming enough lots.

This is only the preliminary stage in a continuous refining process through the various progression of the Settlement. Some lots will be knocked and knocked again between fewer and fewer members until all are satisfied that the goods are 'done' – that is, they cannot be milked any further.

The Settlement itself – usually held in an upstairs room in a country house or in a private room or in a nearby hotel – can be an instrument of either childish simplicity or diabolical complexity, in accordance with the wishes of the participants, rather like a poker school. Just as one may simply play the cards on their merits, or on chance, or on the other players' demeanour, or on bluff and double-bluff, so all these techniques may be used in the KO.

When the Boys are all present, the chairman calls in their sale bills and puts up the lots, working from each bill in turn.

On the chairman's injunction 'Claim it if you want it,' the settlement begins. 'Lot 9 cost £5 . . .' At the end of the proceedings, members place on the table the money bid for each lot they have claimed. This is the Knock money. It is then shared out equally among members.

After the Knock money is shared out (together with any money from the ante-Ring), members who bought the lots at the original sale are repaid whatever they bid by members who have successfully claimed these lots.

But it is always open to the original buyer to say that he wishes to retain the lot, even though he may not have bid in the Knock. If this happens, there is then a limited knock between the original buyer and the new claimant, or perhaps a straight bargain is struck. In either case, the money offered for the lot goes entirely to the dealer relinquishing the goods. One gets either the goods or the money: this is the fundamental principle of the Settlement.

Tactics are important and there are two ways of taking part in the KO. The simplest is to concentrate entirely on obtaining those goods one wishes to buy without worrying unduly about how much Knock money one has to pay in, and to regard the share one receives at the end as contingent discount.

A slightly more sophisticated method is to buy as little as one dare, concentrating on the 'snips' so as to pocket as large a share of the Knock money as possible as a net cash gain. For the lower ranks of the hierarchy, however, this carries the risk of expulsion for 'not wanting the goods'.

Experienced members of the Ring aspire to higher levels of play. They aim to make every lot yield as much Knock money as possible. To this end, they will 'gee up' any lot, whether or not they require it, until in their judgment it can be milked no further.

But just as the Settlement is designed to remove goods from the open competition of the saleroom, so within the Settlement itself there may be an even smaller group of the most knowledgeable and financially powerful dealers who will exclude the smaller fry from the Knock for some lots.

When one of these lots is put up in the Settlement, the top men will not bid against one another. They will wait until the less knowledgeable dealers have finished bidding, and then the chairman will knock it down to one of the top men. This lot is then carried forward to the second Knock, limited to those members who have signified to the chairman that they have a further interest in them.

This refining principle has two advantages. First, it conserves the 'wages' (Knock money) on these lots for those who have the greater knowledge. Secondly, that knowledge is not spread

128

fruitlessly before the eager intelligence of those still to learn.

Once the senior members have withdrawn into the inner court of the second Knock, the cut and thrust becomes keener. The goods to be 'done' are more important, and the sums are in keeping with the status of the members. It now becomes very difficult to distinguish knowledge from bluff. Some of the verbal feinting and probing at this stage would do credit to a professional interrogator.

There may be yet another stage in the proceedings. If a few dealers share a common interest in lots not wanted by most other members of the Settlement, there may be considerable lobbying beforehand to agree to refrain from claiming during the Settlement and to knock privately afterwards, in a sort of post-Ring. This is not encouraged, however. It can create a very sterile Settlement, undermining the institution.

Even if a sale looks disappointing, it may still be possible for the Ring to 'make the wages' by manufacturing a 'set-up' – that is, using 'wrong' lots as a decoy for members of the KO who merely purport to be knowledgeable. A whispered campaign to inspire confidence in the 'wrong' lots will con the victims into hanging on in the Knock. If this trick is successful, the subsequent Knock money can make a trip to a third-rate sale quite profitable.

Occasionally, two different Rings come into action at the same sale. This happens when, say, good quality paintings or perhaps silver and porcelain appear at a country sale. This may attract the notice of leading London dealers, lofty characters who are not in the habit of settling with Tom, Dick and Harry in the country and don't consider the local Knockout a serious threat.

The local dealers, on the other hand, turn out to show that they are a force in their own country who will not allow anyone to take away their 'gear' for nothing. As a result, the auctioneer will have the time of his life, with record prices. This phenomenon angers Ring members more than any other, for it is a negation of their *raison d'être* – and it costs them money, too.

Now here is Bernard Levin's* somewhat simplified account (written before the *Observer* revealed that a 'ring' was now a 'knockout') of an imaginary ring in action:

> The sensational sale, to the National Gallery, of St Paul's Cathedral, for a figure said to be a little over nine billion pounds, has given rise to an extraordinary series of rumours, allegations and gold-plated yachts.
>
> The building was acquired at a small country-house sale by Mr Siegfried Treppengeländer, of Treppengeländer and Spritzwasser, the old-established art-dealers. The price paid at the sale was 16s 4d, and many experts have expressed surprise at the rather low figure, particularly in view of the considerably higher price asked when St Paul's was offered to the nation.
>
> It appears that, although there are a number of old-established Wren specialists who, had they seen the work in question, would instantly have identified it, none of these was actually present.
>
> Several did not receive catalogues; others received catalogues with the vital page missing; others were unaccountably delayed, on their way to the sale, by floods, storms, traffic-jams, knifings, etc.
>
> At the sale itself, it was noticed that there was only one bidder apart from Mr Treppengeländer; this was the old-established village idiot, who dropped out when the price went above 16s, largely because he had received a vigorous blow behind the right ear from a plastic Ming-type statuette.
>
> Afterwards, a number of dealers retired to a suite at a nearby hotel, booked by Mr Treppengeländer, from behind the locked doors of which they could be heard relaxing with cries of 'Forty million quid from the bidder in the corner,' and similar

Daily Mail, 5 November 1968.

expressions of the fellowship and good cheer which exists among old-established art-dealers.

A week later, Mr Crispin Gladhander, of the old-established firm of Marjoribanks and Featherstonehaugh, resigned abruptly – owing to a forthcoming attack of bad health – from the Committee of the British Art Dealers League, to the great regret of the other members, several of whom left the same night for a long-postponed Continental holiday, playfully wearing false beards and blue-tinted spectacles.

Interviewed on the subject, Mr Simon Baldpate, chairman of Ourcut & Co, the old-established auctioneers, expressed great interest in the matter. 'A ring, did you say?' he inquired. 'How extraordinarily fascinating. How do you spell it, now? Dear me, dear me; something to do with Wagner, is it?'

The President of the old-established Board of Trade has called for a full report. Mr Treppengeländer is unfortunately not available for comment, and all inquiries are being dealt with for him by the old-established Lincoln's Inn firm of Marjoribanks, Featherstonehaugh and Gladhander (and, of course Treppengeländer).

The Auctions (Bidding Agreements) Act, which made rings illegal, was passed in 1927. It reads:

> If any dealer agrees to give, or gives, or offers any gift or consideration to any other persons as an inducement or reward for abstaining, or for having abstained, fom bidding at a sale by auction either generally or for any particular lot, or if any person agrees to accept, or accepts, or attempts to obtain from any such dealer any such gift or consideration as aforesaid, he shall be guilty of an offence under this Act, and shall be liable on summary conviction to a maximum penalty of six months' imprisonment and a fine of £100.

So far as I am aware, there has not been a single successful prosecution under the Act. The reason always given for this is that it is virtually impossible to prove that anyone has abstained from bidding. Even so, if a serious effort were ever made by the police in co-operation with the reputable auctioneers and dealers something could be done to reduce the prevalence of this crime. In my own experience the ring-men are so bold that they might easily give themselves away to police officers masquerading as dealers. On one occasion in a London saleroom I was sitting next to a dealer when another dealer, whom he knew only by sight, put a note into his hands and walked away. The note said, 'We are bidding for Lot So-and-so. If you lay off we will settle with you afterwards.' The dealer, who had had no intention of bidding for Lot So-and-so, did not know what to do. He was sufficiently intrigued by the incident to want to find out what was meant by, 'we will settle with you afterwards', but in the event the ring was outbid by someone else and the occasion for settling did not arise. On another occasion, after I had outbid a hastily-formed ring at a small sale, I was approached by one of their number who tried first to sow doubt in my mind about the value of the lot and then offered me a cheque for half the price I had paid in order to share my risk of loss!

I have found that even those people in the art trade whose behaviour is absolutely impeccable are reticent about discussing the activities of the rings. It is as if they feared that by simply admitting that they are aware of a ring's existence they will become contaminated. At the big auction-houses they take the attitude that they do all they can to combat the ring with reserve prices and accurate catalogue information and that, anyway, the menace rarely shows itself in their salerooms.

In November 1964 the *Sunday Times* caused something of a sensation by exposing the activities of a ring of antique dealers concerned in the buying of a superb Chippendale commode at a Leamington Spa sale for £750 – considerably less than a tenth of its retail market value. But much more important than the actual case quoted was the fact that the newspaper's staff showed how successful police action under the 1927 act would be possible. If a *Sunday Times* reporter, armed with a pocket radio-transmitter, was able to bluff his way into the knockout following a major country sale and relay the whole proceedings so that a tape-recording could be made by his accomplices outside, surely the police could have done the same thing long before. From the general discussion that followed this brilliant newspaper investigation the most disturbing evidence that emerged was to the effect that in many cases the rings operate with the connivance of the country auctioneers. This connivance may go much deeper than is apparent in the saleroom to the private buyer who finds his bids being ignored or who, after getting a lot knocked down to him, is told when he tries to collect it that he 'must be mistaken, it is on a dealer's list'. At Christie's and Sotheby's, I have heard many reports of the country auctioneers who, when called in to advise on the disposal of the contents of big houses, try to retain for sale in their own auction-rooms property that would sell much better in a London auction-room. At best this is the understandable fault of a businessman wanting to keep prestige and commission for himself. At worst it is a criminal betrayal, for gain – sometimes a very big gain – of his responsibility to the vendor.

In a case that was being freely talked about in the art trade some years ago a country auctioneer kept back a painting which he later knocked down to the ring at £30. In the ring's knockout it went, for a figure said to be around £2,000 to a dealer who then put it into a London auction-room where it made more than £50,000. In such a case as this a corrupt auctioneer would probably have to resort to some trick to ensure that only those dealers in league with him knew of the existence of the lot. One method is to omit the lot from the catalogue and then introduce it into the sale at the last moment as an 'additional lot'. Another is to omit it from the preview and tell enquirers that it has been temporarily withdrawn. Sometimes it may simply be hung in a dark and inaccessible position. I have been to sales at which evidence suggested that all these tricks were being employed either by the auctioneer or by a porter on his own initiative. A pound or a fiver slipped to a porter will often be enough to ensure that a particular lot is 'lost' until the sale takes place.

Following the *Sunday Times exposé* auction-rings were the subject of a spirited debate in the House of Commons. Cries of 'Commercial brigandage!' 'Crooks!' and 'Parasites!' were heard in the Chamber and the rings were likened, by enthusiastic MPs, to the wartime black market and to Rachmanism. 'The only way to kill these mosquitoes is to drain the swamp in which they breed,' said Mr Ridley (Conservative, Cirencester and Tewkesbury) with fine fervour but without (at least, so far as my newspaper reported him) defining exactly where or what the swamp was and how it was to be drained. The Government promised to examine the question of new legislation on auction sales, but the rings went on more or less as before. So, even today, for those selling property at auction the only safeguard against the rings is still, as it has always been, the reserve price. Fixing the right reserve on a work of art is itself an art. One might say a 'lost' art, for in the inflationary seventies it has become impossible, even for the experienced staff of the major auction-houses, to make anything like accurate estimates of sale prices (and that is what reserve prices should be). So before you decide to take that picture of yours to the nearest auctioneer, find out everything you can about it. Otherwise it might become a 'discovery' for someone else and qualify for inclusion in the next chapter.

8

Snatch Yourself a Treasure

Whereas the millionaire and the rich man may, as things stand at present, form fine collections by sheer power of capital, the poor man has to depend on his wits. Yet the necessity which forces him to be his own expert is not altogether a hard necessity . . . Now and then he may snatch some treasure under the very eyes of dealers and millionaires, or may unearth in some grimy portfolio a drawing for which a fellow could hardly be found outside a royal or national collection

Sir Charles Holmes,
Pictures and Picture Collecting (1903)

One day way back in 1933 my friend Pierre Jeannerat, who was then twenty-one (and was later, for many years, art critic of the *Daily Mail*), was looking around Christie's when he came across a wooden box containing a couple of bronze horses and two Victorian bronze cherubs. Idly picking them up one after the other he realised that one of the horses was of a completely different quality from the other items in the 'job' lot. It was squat and distorted and had nothing of the prettiness of the other horse, but somewhere in his memory it rang a bell. He studied it closely, holding it at different angles in his hands until suddenly he realised what it was that it had evoked in his memory – Leonardo da Vinci's many drawings of rearing horses that he had seen at Windsor Castle, studies for *The Battle of Anghiari,* for *St George and the Dragon,* and for the Trivulzio Monument. Hardly daring to hope that he had discovered a hitherto unknown bronze by the great Florentine master, he left the saleroom and began a feverish search for every bit of information he could find about Leonardo's sculpture and when the day of the sale arrived he was convinced that the horse was a study for the Trivulzio Monument. But had anyone else come to a similar conclusion? The tension as he waited for the lot number to be called was almost unbearable. He knew that, if any dealer felt as he felt about the horse, he could not hope to get it. The highest sum he could possibly afford to bid was fifty pounds, little more than the lot would be worth if all the bronzes were Victorian. He waited in an agony of suspense that justifies every cliché. The bidding started at one guinea and at eleven and a half guineas the lot was knocked down – to him.

For years afterwards he was almost alone in believing that his horse was by Leonardo but slowly experts throughout the world began to consider his claim seriously and in 1961 his faith in his own judgment was seen to be fully justified when the horse was included in the major exhibition of Italian bronze statuettes held at the Victoria and Albert Museum. It was listed as by Leonardo in the catalogue, which included this description of it by the eminent authority, John Pope-Hennessy:

The statuette forms one of a group of three horses by or after Leonardo, of which the most celebrated is a *Riding Warrior* at Budapest and the second is in the Metropolitan Museum of Art, New York. The horses are the only works of sculpture that can be directly associated with Leonardo, and certainly depend from models by this artist. It has been claimed that both the present bronze and that at Budapest are preparatory studies for Leonardo's Trivulzio Monument, but, as noted by Clark, their closest affinities in Leonardo's work are with the drawings for the fresco of the *Battle of Anghiari,* and it is likely that they are casts from wax models for the fresco by Leonardo, and were made in Florence *c.* 1508.

The story of Jeannerat's horse, which is worth a fortune today, is of the sort that makes us all ask ourselves, 'Why can't I find a masterpiece?' If we are to judge by newspaper reports one such discovery is made almost every day. 'Painting in cupboard may be an art treasure', '£1 picture is a Rembrandt', 'Cleaned-up painting may be worth £100,000' read the headlines, but nine times out of ten no more is heard about these spectacular finds. The late Sir Albert Richardson, a former President of the Royal Academy and therefore a man who ought to have known better, repeatedly made news with reports of his sensational discoveries. I have no doubt he did find many worthwhile pictures for he was knowledgeable about art and an assiduous explorer of junk and antique shops, but wishful thinking, the arch-enemy of true scholarship played far too big a part in his searches and research. He relied entirely upon his own judgment and was contemptuous of that of others who disagreed with him.

Once when I went to see him at his home in Ampthill he had just discovered a new 'Gainsborough', a version of the National Gallery's famous picture of the artist's daughters chasing a butterfly. When I dared to suggest that it could be a good Victorian copy he said 'It's the Victorian frame. Fooled everybody, but not me.' Had he, I asked, taken it to the National Gallery for verification? 'It's not safe there,' he joked (it was shortly after Goya's *Duke of Wellington* had disappeared from the Gallery). I was taken on a conducted tour of the house which was like an antique shop in which the good and the indifferent jostled on equal terms. He was like Aladdin in the magic cave. He opened a door and exclaimed, 'There's *Mrs Fitzherbert* by Gainsborough! And look at those – Constable, Wouwerman, Greuze, Hogarth, he painted it in an hour for a bet, and Vernet, an original Vernet! And there! An Egg! And that – a Swebach des Fontaines, the only one in England! Oh, and look at our dear friend Ford Madox Brown under a Teniers. And see those? Rubens, Fisher Prout, and Rushbury all together!' Then he dashed ahead to another room and started the spiel all over again. 'That's a Van Goyen and this is a Claude. Here's a Wilson and this is Benjamin West's *St James's Park*. Chardin, Opie, Girtin, a very early Constable, Lépine, Cundall – it all mixes, see?'

After my comments on the 'Gainsborough' I was given no opportunity to study any of the other pictures closely to see if they all justified Sir Albert's enthusiasm. But two months after my visit the following newspaper reports appeared:

SIR ALBERT GOES NAP

He has done it again! For the fifth time in six months Professor Sir Albert Richardson has identified an unknown picture as a valuable work by a great artist.

The 81-year-old professor went to lunch with my colleague Jimmy Wentworth Day, gazed at a picture on the dining-room wall and announced: 'You've got a genuine Reynolds there.'

SNATCH YOURSELF A TREASURE

He was right.

How does it happen that Sir Albert has found quite so many pictures lately?

'Oh, I don't know,' he said with a shrug. 'But I haven't been collecting pictures for sixty years for nothing, you know.'

Tomorrow the picture, *The Education of Love,* goes up for sale at Sotheby's.

I'm hoping for a five-figure sum,' says Wentworth Day. The picture has been in his family for many years, but its painter has remained a mystery until now.

(*Daily Mail,* 30 January 1962)

UNSOLD PICTURE

It must have been disappointing for the owner of the picture attributed to Reynolds when it failed to find a buyer at Sotheby's this week and was bought in for £30.

But the man who spotted it as a Reynolds, Sir Albert Richardson – that architect with a flair for finding Old Masters – is not perturbed. The picture is a copy of a painting by Titian and Sir Albert tells me it is of no great value.

'It is one of a number of sketches Reynolds did as a student in Italy,' says Sir Albert. 'But it is unquestionably by Reynolds. It came from Wentworth Woodhouse and had been in the owner's family for years.'

(*Evening Standard,* 3 February 1962)

What both stories omitted to say was that Sotheby's did not by any means agree that the picture was 'unquestionably by Reynolds'. It was catalogued as 'Reynolds', which, as we all know now, meant that Sotheby's thought it was, at best, by a follower of dear old Sloshy Slosh (as his less respectful students used to call Sir Joshua).

I always thought that wishful thinking was a bad thing because it was inimical to research, but that was before I became involved with a man who combined the two things with such fanaticism that he made my life (and probably his own) a misery for two years. It began in 1970 when I sold a little bronze figure, that I had bought for £25 from a country dealer who told me it was a French eighteenth-century 'river god'. In fact it was a version of Michelangelo's figure of *Day* in the Medici tomb at Florence, but it varied from the huge original in that the figure reclined on an almost flat base instead of a steeply curved architrave. This unusual feature probably escaped the Sotheby's young lady, who took a one-second glance at it and said, as if she saw one every day, 'It's nineteenth century. They fetch about sixty-five pounds.' But I liked it more than £65 and kept it.

About a year later I met a general dealer from British Columbia who was in London trying to sell a 'four-million-dollar' collection (called the Lebrooy Collection, of Montreal) of 'Michelangelo' terra-cottas. After seeking the advice of Peter Wilson of Sotheby's he asked me to introduce him to Wilden-stein's. But no one, he told me later, took him seriously. 'You only have to mention Michelangelo here and everyone thinks you're mad', he complained. In fact he knew a lot about Michelangelo and when I showed him my little bronze he snapped it up – for £65. Then he went back to Canada and I forgot him until before dawn one Sunday the telephone frightened me out of a beautiful dream. The Canadian had decided that the bronze was a cast from a little-known terracotta by Michelangelo in the Museum of Fine Arts, Houston, Texas. If I would help him by digging up the bronze's history he would cut me in for five per cent of the proceeds of its sale.

For the next few months I was bombarded with documents

and photographs and catalogues which established that the Canadian, like Hamlet, was only mad north-north-west – he could tell a Michelangelo from a handsaw. The Houston Museum did own a terracotta of *Day* the same size as the bronze and closely resembling it, except that the left foot was missing.

From this material I learned that this terracotta and the fifteen smaller pieces in the Lebrooy Collection had a documented history that went back to the sixteenth century, and that as part of the von Praun Collection for 260 years from about 1580, and, as part of the Hähnel Collection in the nineteenth century, they had been famous. As late as 1913, when the German art historian, Henry Thode prepared a catalogue of them for the Hähnel family he considered most of them to be from the hand of the great master. Later they passed to a Dr A B Heyer who, as a refugee from Germany, brought them with him to England.

Poor Dr Heyer, whoever he was! On 24 February 1938 (where were you and I on that day?) his wonderful collection came up at Christie's in a (predominantly) furniture sale and the whole lot (thirty-two pieces in twenty-six lots) fetched £362.15.6d! The Houston figure realised the top price – £105. Most of the items now in the Lebrooy Collection fetched less than three guineas each – including five which the Michelangelo authority, Ludwig Goldscheider maintains are authentic. The others are, presumably, by *'garzoni di Michelangelo'* and, of course, of no mean value.

Fascinating, but it threw no light upon the Canadian's bronze *Day*. The problem of who made it, and when, still baffled me until one day in the Brtish Museum I read that Professor Hähnel had been Professor of *Sculpture* at the Dresden Academy. Had he, or one of his pupils made the bronze by copying or taking a mould from the terracotta (and adding the flat plinth and, maybe, a foot)? I put this idea up to the Canadian (in spite of the fact that it would reduce my five per cent to peanuts) but he brushed it aside and went on with his research. He was prepared to go to the ends of the earth (and almost did) to prove that the bronze was an early cast made from the terracotta and that the terracotta was by the great master. He did not give up when he was told in Houston that the terracotta was now attributed to Michelangelo's pupil, Tribolo, and that, even if the bronze had been cast from it, it was a very late cast, nor when three experts at the Victoria and Albert Museum all concurred in the opinion that it was nineteenth century.

He travelled, at a cost of thousands of dollars, to Houston, London, Paris, Dresden, Munich, Vienna, Prague, and other places far from his home. Finally, two years after the saga began, he came up with what he thought was conclusive proof that the bronze was what he wanted it to be. He had found a German art publication dated 'Leipzig 1876' in which was an illustration of the *Day* (complete with two feet and an added plinth) described as a 'terracotta sketch by Michelangelo in the possession of Professor Hähnel in Dresden'. Unfortunately the illustration was clearly not of the Houston terracotta but of a plaster cast, for it showed distinctly the joins of the piece-mould in which it had been made. Evidently Professor Hähnel, not wishing to trust the photographer with the original terracotta, had given him a plaster replica instead. Experts at the Victoria and Albert Museum and the Houston Museum both confirmed that the illustration was of a plaster cast and from this it seemed sensible to conclude that it was Hähnel the sculptor who had

had the bronze figure made, some time between about 1850, when the terracotta came into his possession, and 1876. Comparison even between the photographs of the plaster and the bronze show how (as in the case of a forger) even a bronze-finisher, and especially a nineteenth-century one, cannot conceal the fact that he is a man of his own time. Too much chasing and polishing has dissipated most of the feeling of latent power and strength that emanates from the terracotta and even from the plaster cast.

Unfortunately my Canadian friend could not accept these conclusions. How, he asked, could the photograph be of a plaster cast when the article states that it is of the actual terracotta model? During twenty-five years in journalism I asked myself that sort of question at least once every week.

As you will have gathered, my knowledge of sculpture is somewhat limited and I might easily have let a 'real' Michelangelo bronze slip through my fingers. But I made no mistake the day I bought four bronzes by Henry Moore for eight pounds. It happened in August 1968, during the 'close season' at Sotheby's and Christie's, when I wandered into the salerooms of Puttick & Simpson (now affiliated with Phillips) and rummaged through the properties to be sold the following day under the ambiguous heading 'Chinese Porcelain, Bronzes etc'. In a shallow wooden box of the sort used for potting-plants and marked in chalk 'Lot 39' I found a bronze bust of President John Kennedy, signed F (for Fredda) Brilliant, and four bronze figures, all signed 'Moore' and identical except for the numbers 1/9, 4/9, 5/9, and 6/9 alongside the signatures. Quickly replacing them in the box, in case anyone should see what I had discovered, I went in search of a sale catalogue and read: '39. *A head of a young man, and four bronze shells'*.

It was unbelievable. Waiting until there were no other viewers in the room, I went back to the box and took another quick look. There was no mistake. The 'Moores' were undoubtedly *Henry* Moores. The description of them in the catalogue was partly correct, for in making them the sculptor had evidently taken a clam shell and added to it a typical Moore-ish head and torso.

While I was standing there pretending to be absorbed in the catalogue, but in fact praying that no one else had seen, or would see, what I had seen, an art-dealer, a little man who has a little gallery not far from the saleroom, came in. Clearly this was not one of his regular haunts any more than it was mine. He made a quick general survey of the scene, a perfunctory examination of a few plates, rubbed a hand absentmindedly over the rump of a bronze *Gleaner* signed 'Dalou', and then came to a halt in front of Lot 39. I watched him put his hand in the box, push the 'shells' around a bit and then pick up the head of Kennedy – and put it down again. Then he moved on to Lot 38, 'four bronze figures', examined them closely and presumably saw, as I had seen, that they were by George Ehrlich, RA. He pulled a wry face – they were not the best of Ehrlich – and left the room. I left too. It was almost time for the saleroom to close and few more people were likely to view.

But how many had viewed before me? And how many of these had recognised the Moores? And how many of those who recognised them knew how much they were worth? And how many of those who knew what they were worth had the money to pay for them? I certainly had not. I estimated that, at Sotheby's or Christie's they would fetch at least £1,000 each and I decided to bid up to £2,000 and worry about raising the money afterwards.

Next morning I arrived at the saleroom with a quarter of an hour to spare. Almost the first face I saw (it was the only face I recognised) was that of a fellow art-critic-cum-sales-reporter. Then began (or so it seemed to me) a nervous game of cat and mouse between us, each trying to find out what the other was after, each pretending he was there just in the line of duty, to 'see how things go'. Then he asked me what I thought of the Dalou *Gleaner,* and I told him, honestly, that I thought it was probably genuine but not a very good cast, and that it would probably fetch around £100. We looked at it together for about half a minute and then, just as the auctioneer appeared, he said, 'I don't think there's anything here for me'. And he left. 'Cunning', I thought. 'He'll suddenly reappear in the doorway just as lot 39 comes up.'

There were about fifty prospective buyers in the room and I did not know one of them, which was encouraging because at that time, I knew, at least by sight, every London art-dealer worth knowing. I sat at the back of the room where I could see everyone who might bid and anyone who might arrive late. At the front, just below the auctioneer's rostrum, was a green baize-covered table on which the lots were displayed as they came up and at which four or five men, whom I took to be antique-dealers, sat handling, and passing from hand to hand each item as it appeared. They were a motley lot of items – art-nouveau-ish looking vases and lamps, Staffordshire figures, pewter plates, pottery wall-plaques, spelter horses, and of course, some undistinguished-looking bits of Chinese porcelain – none of them of any interest to me. Never did an auctioneer seem so slow (he was, in fact, very quick). Never did a thirty-ninth lot seem so long a-coming (in fact it came in less than twenty minutes).

I affected an air of indifference but I was listening carefully to catch the lot numbers and watching the door where, surely, the little-dealer-with-the-little-gallery and the art-critic were bound to appear at any moment. The 'Dalou' bronze came up and was knocked down for £110. Another five minutes and the auctioneer was saying, 'Lot 38. One pound, anybody?' I did not really want them, but when the bidding stopped at £6 I put up my hand and the four Ehrlich bronzes were mine for £7. 'lot 39' said the auctioneer, and a porter put the wooden box on to the green baize table. He stood the 'Head of a young man' on it and handed the 'bronze shells' to the dealers sitting at the table. As the bidding rose, hesitantly, from one pound to five, I could not take my eyes off the four baffled dealers at the table as they passed the Moore bronzes from hand to hand and hazarded wild guesses as to what the hell they were. Then suddenly I realised the auctioneer was saying, for the third time, 'At seven pounds then.' I waved my catalogue wildly, completely forgetting the need for secrecy and caution. 'At eight, to a bidder at the back,' said the auctioneer, pointing in my direction. 'At eight pounds, then.' A moment's pause, a bang, and, 'Your name please, sir?' I had my card ready for this moment and passed it to a porter. As he handed it up to the clerk of the sale the next lot was already on the green baize table and the auctioneer was already taking bids. No one but I in the room had the slightest idea of what had just happened. To this day I wonder who it was who bid up to seven pounds. Presumably he, or she, wanted the head of President Kennedy.

I left the sale immediately and returned in the afternoon when most buyers had collected their purchases and carried them off. I had horrible thoughts that the Moores might have been stolen from the box, or that someone was going to tell me that a horrible mistake had been made and that I could not have them. But they had not, and no one did. There was, however, a brief moment of alarm for me as I was pushing the bronzes into my brief case. Two acquaintances, members of that army of unsuccessful actors and professional men who supplement their limited incomes by dabbling in a little tax-free dealing, approached me (God knows what they were doing there in the first place) and asked to see what I had bought. 'Just a few crummy bronzes,' I said, speedily stuffing the last of the shell figures into the bag. They smiled patronisingly as I tucked the head of Kennedy under my arm and said goodbye to them.

On my journey home I had plenty of time to reflect upon my good fortune. It had, of course, occurred to me from the start that it was strange that four Henry Moore bronzes, all the same, should have found their way into such a sale, but I had decided that there would be plenty of time to ask questions after I had bought them. That there were questions to ask, my conscience had no doubt, but I could not help arguing with myself that if I had paid say, £4,000 for Lot 39, I would have had no such feeling. There were, however, several reasons why my argument did not convince me. The chief one was that none of the four Moore figures was mounted. The fact that they stood up very well without bases, and that I preferred them that way, was irrelevant.

Next day I put one of the bronzes into my pocket and went to call on Marlborough Fine Art, Moore's dealers, in Old Bond Street. A young woman, thinking I had come to review the exhibition, gave me a complimentary catalogue and I was just about to ask her if I might see the gallery manager when I saw it – a figure just like mine, except that it was mounted on a black wooden base – displayed exactly opposite the entrance to

149

the gallery. From the catalogue I learned that its correct title was *Figure – Shell Skirt* and that it was numbered 2/9. I went through the motions of looking at the rest of the exhibition, and then left.

I had decided that it would be better to see Henry Moore, whose home is only a few miles from mine, himself but he was in Italy and I had to wait a month. During that time I tried to find out who had put the bronzes into the sale. The auctioneers refused, as is usual, to give me the vendor's name and address, but offered to forward a letter from me to her. She was, they said, an old and valued customer. I wrote the letter and waited. About a week later a woman telephoned me and announced, in a very breezy manner, that she was 'Molly H-, MBE' –you'll find me in the London phonebook; I'm well-known in these parts.' She understood, she said, that I wanted to know something about the bronzes she had sold at Puttick & Simpson's.

'Well, yes,' I said. 'I wondered if you could tell me anything about their history?'

'I can only tell you where I bought them – from a little man named Ben in the Portobello Road. You probably know him. He clears houses.'

I confessed that I did not have the good fortune to know Ben, the clearer of houses.

'I gave him twenty pounds for them,' she volunteered. And as I was thinking 'Poor woman, she's lost money on them. If only she could guess what they are', when she added, 'Did you notice some of them were signed "Moore"? I did think they would fetch more. My husband says they should have done.'

The unintentional pun went unremarked by both of us. I made noises of commiseration and she replied, 'Ah well, if there's anything else you want to know just give me a ring. Glad to help. Goodbye!'

During the weeks that passed before Henry Moore telephoned me and asked me to go to see him, the possibility that the bronzes had been stolen at some stage before they reached 'Ben' began to look more and more like a probability. In spite of this, several art-dealers, to whom I told the story, offered to pay up to £1,000 for each of the bronzes and 'take a chance that they were all right'.

If I was at all tempted by any of these offers, the temptation did not last long, for I later discussed the legal position with a solicitor friend who had acted for one of several innocent purchasers concerned in a notorious case of a stolen painting by Munnings. From this precedent it was clear that if I were to sell a bronze for, say, £1,000, to a dealer who later sold it to a client for £1,500, I would, in the event of the bronze being proved to have been stolen, be liable to refund to the dealer not only the purchase price of £1,000 but also his lost profit of £500!

When I finally went to see the sculptor he made me recount to him (and his family) the whole of my story before he revealed that the bronzes had, in fact been stolen, six months earlier from the foundry where his smaller works are cast. He then confessed that the burglary, evidently by ignorant metal-thieves, had never been reported to the police – a fact that, I believe, would have put a completely different legal complexion upon my possession of them.

Fortunately, this was the only find I have made that proved to be stolen. But I always wonder how such things as the large oil painting by Christian Rohlfs that I bought for £1 at Knight, Frank & Rutley's saleroom (where it was catalogued 'Modern School') and the twenty-two Géricault drawings (catalogued as

151

Lord Leighton) that I did not buy at Bonham's because a friend forgot to bid for me, still get into minor sales. Before such things can become 'discoveries' they have to be 'lost', at least in the sense that their owners don't know what they are.

In spite of all that is written about art today, in spite of all the opportunities available to everyone to see and appreciate great art, the feeling for it (as distinct from its money value) is still a very rare thing. Most people, no matter what their standards of general education, are not moved by paintings, even great ones. So it is that important pictures are often brought to the salerooms by their owners who are unaware that the picture they have lived with for decades is a masterpiece and worth a fortune.

In December 1969 Sotheby's sold, for £224,000, an unrecorded work, *The Temptation of Eve,* by the rare German master, Hans Baldung 'Grien' (*c.* 1484-1545), a painting that combines extraordinarily beautiful form and design with such horrible imagery that living with it would, one imagines, be a daily hell, with all its delights and horrors. But it was taken to Sotheby's by an Edinburgh art-teacher, Mrs V G Cattrell, in whose family it had been for three generations, and it had always been attributed to the 'school of Lucas Cranach'. Before the current art boom it was valued at £20, but when Mrs Cattrell decided to sell it she hoped to get enough to pay the deposit on a new car. The painting is now in the National Gallery of Canada.

In July 1972, again at Sotheby's, a completely unknown early Gainsborough masterpiece, *Mr and Mrs John Gravenor and their daughters, Elizabeth and Dorothea,* fetched £280,000. It also had been for generations in the family of the vendors, two middle-aged sisters, who had always understood it was a fake or

a copy and only jokingly referred to it as 'the family Gainsborough'. In the 1930s the picture was valued for insurance at
£1,500. For sixteen years before it was sold it hung in the
dining-room of the home at Hythe, Kent, of one of the sisters.
And yet, until a young man from Sotheby's was bowled over by
it at first sight, none of the scores of visitors who must have
been in that dining-room were ever, it would seem, conscious
of being in the presence of a dazzling manifestation of genius.
So much for our art-enlightened age.

But of all such stories the most outrageous is that of the huge
Daniel in the Lion's Den by Rubens, a 7 ft by 10 ft canvas,
which turned up at Bonham's saleroom, London, in 1963, was
bought *before* the sale for £500, and next appeared in 1966 on
the walls of the National Gallery, Washington, which had paid
more than £178,000 for it. This picture, one of the few large-
scale works known for certain to have been painted by the
master without the help of his assistants, had been well known
to every Rubens scholar for three centuries. Its history from the
time it was painted in 1615, was fully recorded. Bought as soon
as it was dry by Sir Dudley Carleton, British Ambassador at the
Hague, it was given by him to King Charles I and after that it
was in the collection of the Dukes of Hamilton for more than
two hundred years. In 1873 it was shown in an exhibition of
Old Masters at the Royal Academy and the Academy's label,
stuck on the back at that time and clearly identifying it –
Rubens, 'Daniel In the Lion's Den', proprietor Duke of Hamilton
– was still on it while it was at Bonham's. From the 13th Duke
of Hamilton it passed to the Cowdray family in 1919 and it was
the present Lord Cowdray who sent it to Bonham's. For some
time it had cluttered up the old-fashioned offices in London of
his family holding company, Whitehall Securities. So when, in

1963, the company moved to the newly completed Millbank Tower skyscraper it was cleared out, said Lord Cowdray (who had always believed it was only a copy), 'with a lot of other stuff we didn't need'.

What happened thereafter was racily reported three years later in the *Sunday Times**:

> The painting, with two other 'boardroom pictures' was sent by carriers to Bonham's auction rooms in Knightsbridge. Garth Lawson, Bonham's high-speed picture expert ('I must attribute something like 25,000 pictures a year'), was daunted by the jumbo-sized canvas.
>
> It would, he thought, 'spoil the view of a nice little sale'. He noticed the yellowing RA label on the back but was not much impressed.
>
> After some thought, he decided the figure was by Jordaens – 'He always painted stumpy legs.' Two dealer friends also opined that it was no Rubens: they plumped for a modest painter called De Voss†. Lawson did not speak to any accepted Rubens scholars.
>
> Thus, the Old Master re-emerged catalogued as Lot 25 for the August 1 1963, sale at Bonham's with the attribution to Jordaens and De Voss. A footnote added that it had once been attributed to Rubens.
>
> Even this curious description, however, would not have deterred the practised Rubens-spotters had they been given the chance to see it. But on July 22, a few days before the catalogue went out, a photograph of Lot 25 was sent round to Julius Weitzner, a man with a reputation for buying massive religious paintings and placing them with American institutions. ('Strictly Old Testament stuff. My main clients are kinda Baptist-minded'). Weitzner, an engaging, glad-handing operator, is also a good judge of Rubens: he recently purchased one

*11 September 1966

†Cornelis de Voss (1584-1651) occasionally assisted Rubens.

that had hung, unnoticed for years, on the walls of an Essex pickle factory.

Soon after he received the photograph, Weitzner called Lawson. 'That De Voss,' he said. 'What's it going to fetch?' Lawson thought around £200. 'So,' said Weitzner, 'I'm off abroad in a few days. I'll make you a staggering offer, I'll give £500 for it now.' Bonham's got in touch with Whitehall Securities, who, according to Lawson, were 'tickled pink'.

On July 24, Weitzner stopped by Bonham's and took a quick look at the picture [it was standing at the top of the stairs, I am told, too big to get into the saleroom] before it was consigned to America.

A day later, the Bonham catalogue, with its illustration of Lot 25, started pouring into the letterboxes of other dealers. All over Europe the phones started ringing. The established London dealers, Leggatt's, Agnew's and Knoedler's all rang Jaffé (this country's leading Rubens authority) with the same question: 'Isn't that *the* Rubens? Jaffé thought that it almost certainly was. But when Jaffé went down to Bonham's he was told with some brevity that the picture was 'not available'.

In common with many people, he concluded that it had been spotted and withdrawn by the owners. In fact it was already on the high seas without the Reviewing Committee on the Export of Works of Art knowing a thing about it. Exporters of old paintings are only required to apply for a special licence (which can be refused if a work is considered of national importance) when the value exceeds £1,000.*

Weitzner considered that the De Voss *Daniel* was worth no more than he had paid for it – and was therefore exempt from the licence requirement. 'At that time,' he said, 'I could not know that it was a Rubens.'

Weitzner eventually got round to taking a long look at his acquisition some four months later in New York. He rapidly decided that it was not for his big-religious-picture market, and

*Today this is £3,999.

entered into an 'arrangement' with Knoedler's in New York, the mother house of the Knoedler's in St James's, London, to place the picture and check its attribution. They soon ascertained that it was indeed the Rubens.

Jaffé suggested to Weitzner that he should, once the Rubens attribution was unquestioned, bring the picture back to Britain and then formally apply to re-export it. Weitzner considered this a very curious proposal.

But overt hostilities did not break out until late in 1965 when negotiations between Knoedlers and the National Gallery in Washington were at an advanced stage. Sir Philip Hendy (then Director of the National Gallery, London) sent a sharp telegram advising against the sale. He cited 'alleged irregularities' over the picture's export. But it was a vain rearguard action.

Garth Lawson – whose last word on the affair was, 'I thought it was a horrible picture in 1963, and it is a horrible picture now' – left Bonham's shortly after that article was published and set up as a dealer in London's West End for a few years. Later he returned to picture cataloguing, for Coe's auction-rooms, and while in this job he was killed in a motoring accident.

Although I first saw the great *Daniel* in 1966 (when I went to Washington for the launching of the American edition of *The Art Game*) I had made the acquaintance of the remarkable Mr Weitzner earlier that year. The occasion was a loan exhibition of Baroque paintings held in the gallery I had just opened in Cambridge and organised by undergraduates, including Prince Richard of Gloucester and Richard Herner, a friend of Weitzner's. There were many fine things in the exhibition but the centrepiece was the 'pickle-factory Rubens', mentioned in the *Sunday Times* report, which Mr Weitzner had recently bought for a few pounds. It was a big, ugly picture of St Sebastian to which I, and most who saw it, immediately took a dislike. A well-painted figure of the saint was surrounded by some of the ugliest angels I have ever seen. They were so badly drawn that, had the work not been vetted by the famous Michael Jaffé, who had decided it was an unfinished composition by the master,* I would have said it could not possibly be by Rubens. (In fact, I did say it, but not to Mr Jaffé or Mr Weitzner).

After the exhibition ended I never saw the picture again until June 1970 when it turned up in a sale of Important Old Masters at Sotheby's. It was given a full-page illustration and catalogued with the artist's name in full, Sir Peter Paul Rubens. But on the day of the sale it aroused virtually no interest and was bought in at £800! No dealer of any repute had raised a finger to get the picture. Could it be that Jaffé, Weitzner, and Sotheby's were all wrong? Or was it simply that the dealers found the picture so unattractive as to be unsaleable? I think not. Any picture, however ugly, will still command a considerable price if it is indisputably by a master of Rubens's calibre. Clearly none of the dealers 'believed in' the *St Sebastian.*

I remember the first time a dealer told me, very gently, that he didn't 'believe in' a picture of mine. That, too, was at Sotheby's at a moment that ought to have been a triumph. I was at the 'Impressionist and Modern' sale of 30 June 1966, simply as an observer but when the auctioneer, Peter Wilson, had difficulty in getting anyone to start bidding on Lot 96 at £50, I put up my hand. I had a report to write for an evening newspaper and I hoped in this way to hasten the end of the sale. The picture was familiar to me. It was catalogued: *Alfred de Dreux, 'L'Étudiant à la Chasse', signed* and it had an excellent

*See M Jaffé, *Van Dyck's Antwerp Sketchbook,* 1966, Vol I, pl XVI, and Vol II, p 221.

157

provenance. I had last seen it three years earlier when it was sold at Sotheby's for £400 in one of the seven sales comprising the property of the American multi-millionaire grain-merchant, René Fribourg, so there was little chance that it would be knocked down for less than that three-year-old price. But it was. After trying for more than a minute to coax a further bid the auctioneer, who was clearly as puzzled as I was, knocked it down to me.

Naturally I was delighted. But after I had collected the picture I asked a dealer friend, who specialised in French nineteenth-century pictures, why he did not bid for it, and he replied, 'I didn't believe in it.' That was the moment when I ought to have returned my 'De Dreux' to Sotheby's who, at that time had a condition of sale which said that if, within three weeks, the purchaser showed that there was 'serious doubt as to the authenticity of the lot' he would get his money back. Instead, I chose to keep it. It was not until later that it dawned on me that the previous owner must have sold the picture without putting any reserve price on it, and that that itself was itself 'suspicious'. I looked up the catalogue of the Fribourg sale and found that it included three other De Dreux paintings which had sold for £7,800, £1,800, and £450. All three were illustrated and the photographs showed that only the £450 one closely resembled my picture in technique. The artist might have been in a hurry when he painted them (a pair knocked off quickly for an impatient client?), or he might have had in-digestion. Or again, they might have been the work of a slick copyist or even deliberate fakes. To this day I do not know for sure, but I know I was lucky not to have paid a lot more than £50 for the lesson the experience taught me.

It was somewhat ironical that I made this error less than a

year after the publication of *The Art Game,* in which I was presumptuous enough to lecture my readers on how to avoid making such mistakes. 'If you are thinking of spending any appreciable sum on a painting at a sale' (I wrote) 'give all the time you can to finding out exactly what it is you are going to buy. View the picture on the first possible occasion and use the rest of the time before the sale to ask questions about it and look up reference books. Even where you are quite happy about a picture's authenticity do it just the same. The salerooms are the best free universities there are for an education in the art game and the knowledge you gain there over the years will be invaluable.'

In the years since I gave that advice so many new people, some of them very bright, have moved in on the game that it is now much more difficult to make 'discoveries', even modest ones. But it is possible and the secret is still, I believe, for the gamesman to develop 'taste'. I know that today almost any old rubbish will sell and that many dealers make a fat living out of buying and selling that rubbish. The fact remains that in order to make a habit of discovering *good* things one must develop a general taste for what is good in art. The next step is to develop a special taste for what is good in a particular small field, in short to make oneself a specialist. Such tastes can be acquired just as a taste for wine is acquired, only more cheaply. That is what museums and public art-galleries are for. Anyone who regularly (especially while young and still impressionable) frequents such places as the National Gallery, the Victoria and Albert and the British useums, and really looks at the things there, will unconsciously develop a feeling for quality.

This is not, of course, the whole of the story. Once you have found something that your taste tells you is good then you must know what price to pay for it. Sometimes the price may be so small that you can snap the thing up without another thought. At others, although the price asked may be far below the true value of the object it is still more than you can possibly afford. But most times you will be discovering something you feel is good but whose money value is an unknown quantity. This is your biggest problem, for in this case you must pay up before you can do the research that will prove if you have made a money-making discovery.

There is only one way to meet this problem – haunt the salerooms, view everything worth viewing that is in your line and go to the sales and see what they fetch. During the years in which I was paid to go to all the London art sales and write them up for half a dozen different publications, I developed a photographic memory in which I stored up, involuntarily, images of thousands of pictures, each with a price-tag and a sale-date on it. I felt a bit like the persecuted hero of Elias Canetti's extraordinary novel, *Auto da Fé*, who carried the whole of his library around in his brain and, every night, had to take it out and carefully stack it before he could go to sleep. Unfortunately my 'library' is out of date now, not only because I no longer go to every sale at Christie's and Sotheby's but because prices shoot up so crazily that yesterday's record price may well be broken today and again tomorrow, and will almost certainly be broken before it gets into the next of those sale-prices indexes (which, incidentally, have always seemed to me to be of little use to anyone who has not *seen* the actual pictures to which the prices apply).

9

The Shotgun
Wedding

If you go into a dealer's you can see something, consider it and then ask your wife and your aunt what they think of it. But in the saleroom a revolver is put to your head. It's now or never. It's a sort of shotgun wedding.

PETER WILSON Chairman of Sotheby's,
in an interview on the BBC Third Programme

In recent years the activities of the art market have been given almost as much prominence in the Press as sporting events, and big sales at Sotheby's or Christie's have filled as many column inches as big fights. It was not always so. It is a post-war phenomenon and even as late as the mid-1950s the big auctioneers and the general public remained virtually unaware of each other's existence. Outstandingly high prices paid in the salerooms had, of course, always rated a few lines down the news pages of the daily papers but these served only to stress the remoteness of the world of art-money from the ordinary newspaper-reader. Fine art auctioneers cared little for publicity of a popular sort. Although they had been disposing of art for money since the eighteenth century both Christie's and Sotheby's preferred to be thought of as art institutions rather than market-places. And since only a minute and *élite* fraction of the public was interested in buying works of art it seemed to them that there was nothing to be gained by having their affairs bandied about. They therefore treated the popular Press with a couldn't-care-less coolness that continued until 1958 when they made a complete *volte face* and began to woo newspapers, magazines, radio and television with all the ardour that modern public-relations methods can simulate.

Why 1958? That was the year of the phenomenal Goldschmidt Sale in which just seven Impressionist and Post-Impressionist pictures were sold at Sotheby's for £781,000.* It was also the year in which Peter Wilson became chairman of the firm. Although still little-loved and largely unwooed, the popular Press showed tremendous interest in the Goldschmidt Sale. The 'madness' of people who could spend such vast sums of money on pictures, and modern pictures at that, was a fitting subject even for those who had never heard of Cézanne or Manet, Renoir or Van Gogh. Never before had any sale – and with it the name of Sotheby's – been so widely talked about.

The new chairman, whose pained remark as he brought down the hammer on the £220,000 Cézanne – 'Will nobody bid any more?' – established him as art-gamesman No 1, saw this as a propitious moment at which to set about changing the firm's public image. He must have perceived that publicity of the most general sort could whip up that covetousness which (as he later pointed out) works so virulently upon the hearts,

*In 1968 a single Impressionist painting, Renoir's *Le Pont des Arts, Paris,* sold for £645,834 ($1,550,000) at Sotheby Parke Bernet, New York.

minds, and purse-strings of collectors. And he must have recognised that he was dealing with a new style of collector who welcomed publicity and who was, in fact, not collecting pictures but self-aggrandisement.

Publicity, then, even of the most popular sort, was seen to be good for business and was therefore to be encouraged. But there was a problem. Although newspaper editors had fallen over themselves to give the story of a three-quarters-of-a-million-pound sale they were unlikely to be impressed by anything less spectacular in the future unless it was presented to them in a very 'newsworthy' form. So it came about that in 1959 Sotheby's appointed a firm of Press and public-relations experts to keep their name in front of the public on television and radio and in every branch of the Press. The outcome was as phenomenal as the Goldschmidt sale itself. The effect of triumphs in the saleroom and publicity triumphs following one upon the other almost continuously quickly made London the undisputed centre of the world art market. Soon, millions of pounds' worth of works of art from other countries, especially in the Americas, were being sent to London to be sold every year. In our own country the name Sotheby's became a household word in even the meanest household. It is a synonym for art at fantastic prices and yet (and this is the most remarkable, and, from the point of view of this book, the most interesting outcome of all the publicity) the image of the firm is no longer unreal to the man in the rush-hour bus or tube train. Since 1960 tens of thousands of people who, in earlier years would have been too overawed to set foot inside the Bond Street saleroom, have gone there to watch, to buy or, most commonly, to sell. Thus a largely new source of considerable income was brought to light – the sale of great quantities of properties from vendors of modest means to buyers of modest means. During the 1972-3 season at Sotheby's and Christie's about sixty per cent of all lots were sold at prices not exceeding £200.

Every day now a procession of optimists, their enthusiasm fired by accounts of fortunes made in the salerooms, may be seen, with brown paper parcels under their arms, converging on the offices of the big auctioneers. As they go in their hopes are high. Soon they will come out with them confirmed or shattered or just brought down to earth. Let us imagine that you are one of them and see what happens.

Your brown paper parcel contains the dark flower painting that has been hanging over your mantelpiece unnoticed for twenty or thirty years. You know it is old because it belonged to your mother and your grandmother before you. It is at least a hundred years old so it must be worth quite a bit, you think (but it does not follow). Perhaps it is worth thousands. You have read in the papers recently about a flowerpiece by someone called Van Huysum that sold for £10,000 and another by another Dutchman called Van der Ast that fetched over £20,000. But no, you won't even hope for so much, even a few hundreds would be nice. Anyway there is no harm in asking. You undo your parcel and show the picture to a girl at the reception desk. She may know a little more about painting than you do but she says, 'I'll get someone from the Old Master department to look at if you'll just wait a moment.'

You wait. Already your hopes are soaring. The Old Master department? So it's an Old Master! You are not quite sure what an Old Master means but you have an idea that all Old Masters are worth a lot of money. You take another look at the picture. Why didn't you see before that it is very beautiful? Look at all

164

the marvellous detail in those leaves! And that ladybird, it looks absolutely lifelike. Your thoughts are interrupted by the arrival of a man from the Old Master department who looks far too well-dressed and young to be an expert.

'Good morning,' he says and glances at your picture. 'You want us to sell this for you?'

'Well, I er . . .' you stammer. 'I wondered if you could tell me what it is?'

'Oh yes,' he says. 'It's very nice. A late one, but attractive'. He takes it over to a light and looks at it more closely for a few seconds and returns. 'It's in good condition and should clean up well.'

'You mean I should have it cleaned?' you ask.

'Oh no. If you want us to sell it leave it as it is. Makes it more intriguing to the buyer. Anyway the dealers like the dirt – it hides the quality of the picture from the non-expert.'

'I see,' you say and then, feeling rather a fool for not knowing the answer yourself you ask, 'Can you tell me who it is by?'

The young man glances at it again.

'Well no, I can't say more than that it's late eighteenth century. But we will be able to give it a name,' he adds cryptically. Then you buck up courage to ask the question that has been uppermost in your mind for days.

'Any idea how much it is worth?' you say with feigned casualness.

The young man, who even in his few years at Sotheby's has seen scores, even hundreds, of Dutch flowerpieces of this period and quality sold, answers immediately:

'Six to eight hundred pounds.'

You don't know whether to be pleased or disappointed.

Even £600 was much more than you had hoped for when you first took the picture off the wall but since then you have dreamed of thousands. But you hide your emotions and tell the young man that you will leave it to be sold. He gives you a receipt, tells you that it will probably be sold in two or three months' time and that a catalogue will be sent to you in good time for you to decide what reserve you wish to put on your picture. You go home and try to forget about it until the day the catalogue drops through your letterbox.

Attached to the catalogue is a form that tells you your picture is lot No So-and-So. You turn up Lot No So-and-So and Read.

VAN HUYSUM

Roses, Delphiniums, Mallow and other flowers in an urn on a stone ledge, with a ladybird and a caterpillar, 26 in by 19 in.

You are very excited. So it is by Van Huysum! Or is it? You suddenly remember what you have read in Chapter Five of this book about methods of cataloguing. 'Van Huysum' means simply that in the auctioneers' opinion it is 'a work of the school or by one of the followers of the artist or in his style'. There is, of course, still a slender chance that they may be wrong and that other experts, among the dealers, may believe that it is by Van Huysum himself and will compete for it at the sale. Perhaps you ought to have shown it to one or two other experts before deciding to sell. You could, for example, have taken it to the National Gallery for an opinion free of charge or had it valued by a professional valuer. Even now you could withdraw it from the sale but that would not make you very popular with the auctioneers. You decide, instead, to telephone the young man you saw at the auctioneer's and discuss with him what reserve price you are going to put on it. Would £600 be about right? you ask. The young man thinks it is too high, suggests four hundred. This depresses you a bit again. Has he gone cold on your picture? No, he just wants to be reasonably certain that it does sell. So do you, but you don't want to give it away. You make a compromise – at £500.

A few days before the sale is due your picture and all the others in 'your' sale (as you have now come to think of it) are put on view. You go along to have a look. It takes some time to find your picture, it looks so much smaller now than it looked at home and they have not hung it in the best possible position. In fact you begin to wonder if anyone will notice it at all. You find there are two more flower-pieces in the sale. One, much smaller than yours and not nearly so pretty (it's all sort of stiff and flattish), is catalogued as by 'Balthasar van der Ast'. The second one is very much like yours but considerably bigger and is catalogued as by 'Jan van Huysum'. As far as you can see it is not in any way better than yours – well, only very slightly anyway – so why didn't they catalogue yours with the artist's name in full? You have a good mind to ask the young man why. In fact you do ask him and he explains very courteously. In the first place the big picture is signed and dated (1740), it comes from an important collection and its history during all but the first twenty or thirty years of its existence is documented. But what is even more important is that the drawing, the design, the colour and the almost miraculous precision of the painting announce immediately that it is the work of a master and that master is Jan van Huysum.

The young man obligingly holds your picture alongside the big one and for a moment you, too, can see that there is a difference. What you thought was the marvellous detail in your picture is not now quite so marvellous. The colour is not so rich or varied as that in the bigger picture, the design is not so intricate, and the handling of the paint is not nearly so assured and alive. In fact, says the young man, your picture was painted at least fifty years after the other one, and about forty years after Van Huysum's death, when there was a vogue for his pictures and they were fetching very high prices. It was probably painted as an honest imitation of a style that was in demand but it might have been done as a fake Van Huysum; it hardly matters now. It is just a very nice flowerpiece by an unknown artist of the late eighteenth or early nineteenth century.

On the day of the sale you arrive early and find yourself a seat where you can see as much as possible of what is going on. A quarter of an hour before the sale is due to start you are still almost alone in the saleroom and are beginning to worry that nobody is going to be at the sale to buy your picture. Ten minutes later the room has filled up and the only seats empty are reserved ones. Most of them are reserved for the dealers, who arrive with only a minute or two to spare. They are mostly well-dressed, indistinguishable from any other sort of businessmen, not at all 'arty'. They have a slightly arrogant air, an air of self-importance like that of theatre critics at a first night. They talk and laugh together like the best of friends but soon their quips and cranks will give way to wanton wiles, nods and becks, and, maybe, wreathed smiles. They are still talking when, precisely at the published time, the auctioneer climbs on to his rostrum and announces without any preamble, 'Lot 1.' A porter holds the lot up to him for inspection and then shows it to the audience.

'Lot 1. Ten pounds?' asks the auctioneer. But no one wants to be the first bidder. 'Five pounds, then?' he asks and then, as someone signals a bid, he asks, 'Five pounds I'm bid'. Now the bids follow fast upon each other, 'Eight – Ten – Twelve – Fifteen – Eighteen – Twenty – Twenty guineas – Twenty-five – Thirty . . .' Finally Lot 1, in which no one seemed interested enough to offer ten pounds at the start, is knocked down for ninety pounds. And you have learned your first lesson: Never let your rivals (or the auctioneer) see how anxious you are to get a particular lot. Sometimes, at the smaller salerooms an excited novice, impatient with an auctioneer who is raising the bidding a pound at a time, will call out much higher bids and so alert others to the fact that he thinks he is on to a good thing. At other times the over-anxious bidder finds he is bidding against himself and the auctioneer has to tell him, 'It's your bid, sir.'

Although it may appear to you that the way in which the auctioneer raises the bids is entirely arbitrary there is usually some method in it. In practice there are no hard and fast rules and the skilful auctioneer will be constantly adapting his method, from lot to lot, in such a way as to get the best possible price. Two main factors govern him, the price he hopes and aims to get and the price at which the bidding starts. If the first bid for Lot 1 in 'your' sale had been ten pounds then the auctioneer would probably have continued raising the price in ten-pound units and sold it for the same final figure in rather shorter time. But if at some point no ten pound advance was forthcoming, the auctioneer would have accepted a smaller advance.

Sotheby's catalogues still (in 1974) contain a 'condition of sale' which reads: *No person shall advance any price less than 25p, or above £10, 50p, and so on in proportion or at such rate as the auctioneer may in his absolute discretion direct,* but the first part of this is an anachronism. The amount of the advance at any stage is entirely at the auctioneer's discretion and at Christie's this is stated categorically in the conditions of sale. There is nothing to stop an 'odd-ball' buyer calling out his own bids at any sale but Sotheby's is the last place in the world where, at even the earliest stages of the bidding, an advance of less than £1 would be accepted. In general a five-per-cent minimum advance is the rule, and in these days of inflated prices £10,000 advances are not all that uncommon.

Since the auctioneer on his rostrum is virtually a god, it pays to study him and learn his ways. Peter Wilson once told me the secret of being a good auctioneer: 'You have to get your audience's confidence and then dominate them – in the nicest possible way, of course.' But as a prospective buyer you must not allow yourself to be dominated, not even in the nicest possible way. Your aims and those of the auctioneer are directly opposed. During the sale he is temporarily the 'enemy' and the more you understand about him the less likely you are to be afraid of him or to be carried away by his charm, eloquence, cunning, or whatever is his particular weapon. When you know him well you will often be able to tell from his manner if you are bidding against a reserve and at what point the reserve has been passed, or whether a lot knocked down has really been sold or has been 'bought in' (the value of this sort of knowledge we shall see later).

Usually the first few lots at any sale are comparatively unimportant items, and your sale is no exception. None of the first dozen lots fetches more than a few hundred pounds but then comes a group of better things headed, 'The Property of a Lady of Title'. Among them is the little flowerpiece by Balthasar van der Ast. 'Lot –' announces the auctioneer, 'the flower-painting by Balthasar van der Ast.' He consults his catalogue and then says, 'I have several bids. I must say five thousand pounds to start.' You can hardly believe it. Five thousand for that little thing that, in your eyes is not nearly as attractive as your own picture? 'Five thousand five hundred, six thousand, six thousand five hundred, seven thousand, seven thousand five hundred, eight thousand, eight thousand five hundred', intones the auctioneer looking first here, then there, without pausing. All the time you are scanning the audience trying to make out who is bidding, but you can see no sign. After the bidding has reached ten thousand pounds you notice that the auctioneer is raising it a thousand at a time, 'Eleven thousand, twelve thousand, thirteen thousand' come in quick succession. Then, after a pause, 'Fourteen thousand.' That time you did see the bidder. Or, rather you saw one of those men you took to be dealers raise his eyebrows to the auctioneer. 'Fifteen thousand.' (You did not see that one because it came from the back of the room. But now the eyebrows are raised again). 'Sixteen thousand.' The auctioneer looks around the room and finds a new bidder. Then to the dealer he says, 'Seventeen thousand'. Again the dealer raises his eyebrows and it is eighteen thousand. Another bid from the back of the room, and it is nineteen thousand. The dealer hesitates. 'Nineteen thousand. Against you,' the auctioneer says to him. This time the dealer leaves his eyebrows where they are and says quietly, 'And five.' It is less than a five-per-cent advance but the auctioneer, who senses that the limit has been reached, accepts it. 'Nineteen thousand five hundred pounds.' He takes a last look round his audience, repeats, 'At nineteen thousand five hundred, then,' brings down his hammer and says the buyer's name for the benefit of his clerk.

171

Now you are very excited. And rightly so for that was a good price (considerably more than the dealer, who knows he can sell it for £22,000, had wanted to pay). It was also a 'textbook' piece of auctioneering to which there was more than met your eye. In the first place the 'Lady of title' was not willing to sell at less than £11,000 and had put a reserve price of that amount on the picture. Then three prospective buyers, who were presumably unable to be at the sale, had made advance bids (Americans call them 'order bids') verbally or by letter or telegram. One of them was for £8,000, a second was for £12,000 and a third was for £15,000. The auctioneer was therefore sure, before the sale began, that the picture would be sold and that it would sell for at least £13,000, ie one bid above the second advance bidder's limit.

In spite of this the auctioneer began the bidding at only £5,000. Being something of a psychologist (as well as a bit of an actor) he reasoned that to begin at £10,000, or even £12,000, as he could fairly have done, might have had an adverse effect on some bidders. He knew, too, that he could excite his audience by a rush of bids rising to more than £10,000 in a matter of seconds, and that such excitement can affect bidders favourably from his point of view. But there was a third reason for starting at a comparatively low figure. Imagine that you had made an advance bid of £8,000 and that you had, after all, been able to attend the sale, what would you have thought if the bidding had begun at a figure higher than your offer? Exactly. So the auctioneer made sure not only that justice was done but also that it was seen to be done. When, as you noticed, he paused at £13,000 he had reached the figure at which the man who had made an advance bid of 'up to £15,000' would have got the picture if there had been no further bids from people present in the saleroom. But, as you saw, there were several.

It may seem odd to you that the auctioneer should have accepted several advance bids one of which made it certain that none of the others could be successful. But this is a reflection of the strict confidence which is exercised where such bids are concerned. A reputable auctioneer will not reveal to an enquirer either the reserve price or the size of any bids already received. He will give an estimate of what the picture will sell for and this should of course, take into account the reserve price if it is already known to him.* In the case of the little Van der Ast the estimate given to anyone who asked was £12,000 to £15,000.

Now, back to the sale where the Van Huysum picture is about to be sold. The bidding starts at only £500 (there are no advance bids and although you think the picture is much more attractive than the last one, Van Huysum is over a hundred years later than Van der Ast and has not the same rarity value), and quickly goes up – £800, £1,000, £1,200, £1,500, £1,800 – to £2,000. Again you can see no one bidding but apparently the auctioneer can. He looks first in your direction, but above your head and then at the clerk. You look behind you (unaware that saleroom etiquette forbids it) but can see nobody there and the awful thought strikes you that he may think *you* are bidding. You sit rigidly still, hardly daring to breathe. You watch the clerk who is staring straight in front of him. He, too, is motionless yet the auctioneer turns to him at every alternate bid. 'Seven thousand', the auctioneer is saying over your head, and then to the clerk, 'Seven thousand two hundred.' The clerk continues to look straight ahead but then, after a moment shakes his head. 'At seven thousand two hundred,' says the auctioneer. He no longer looks over your head but scans the

*But this is not possible unless the seller has agreed a reserve price in good time.

173

whole audience and repeats the figure. Then, hesitantly, he taps his hammer, says something that sounds like Finkelbaum or Hogginbotham and proceeds to the next lot. You look behind you again but there is no one who looks anything like a Finkelbaum or even a Hogginbotham. What has been going on?

Briefly it is this. The picture has been 'bought in' because it did not reach the reserve of £7,500 put on it by the owner against the auctioneer's advice. Finkelbaum or Hogginbotham (or whatever the auctioneer said) was a buying-in name for this sale (different names are used on different days). Each time the auctioneer looked over your head he was 'taking one off the wall' – pretending to take a bid from the non-existent Finkelbaum or Hogginbotham. If, as in this case, there is only one 'real' bidder for a picture the auctioneer will bid in this way until the reserve price is reached. In effect he is bidding for the owner of the picture to ensure that it is not sold below the minimum price stipulated. (To be able to detect when a picture has been bought in can sometimes prove profitable to a dealer or collector. A disappointed would-be vendor is often ready, immediately after the sale, to accept a bargain price offered through the auctioneers). The one 'real' bidder this time was the auctioneer's clerk. If you had watched his hands instead of his face you would have seen that he signalled to the auctioneer by moving one finger almost imperceptibly. The clerk is frequently asked by clients who cannot get to the sale to bid on their behalf. In this case, however, the client was present standing at the back of the room. He had arranged that the clerk of the sale should go on bidding for him until he gave a prearranged signal that meant 'Stop'. The signal? – The removal of his spectacles.

Some people may adopt this surreptitious method of bidding just for the hell of it but for those who, for some reason or other, do not wish to be seen bidding, it is better than placing a fixed-limit bid with the auctioneer. Sometimes clients make such arrangements direct with the auctioneer. One important collector, for example, used to clasp his umbrella in front of him for as long as he was bidding, and then let it slip through his fingers to show that he was giving up. Another would blow his nose to show that he was in the bidding and then blow it again to withdraw.

There are obviously dangers for the bidder in this sort of thing as was discovered by the woman who, having arranged to take off her left glove when she had finished bidding, found that the glove had caught on her engagement ring. It can also put a great strain on the auctioneer, as was demonstrated sensationally at Christie's in March 1965 when Rembrandt's lovely portrait of his son, Titus was sold – but only after a dispute – for what was then a British sale-room record price of £798,000.* On that dramatic occasion I found myself, by chance, right next to Mr Norton Simon, the American canned-food tycoon who bought the picture, and I had a close-up of exactly what happened.

For the first hour and a half of the sale Mr Simon sat watching the proceedings and occasionally asking his neighbour, London art dealer (the late) Dudley Tooth, questions about the pictures and the prices. I took him to be an American tourist sightseeing in the saleroom and was surprised when he began to bid for Lot 101, Hogarth's *A Family Party*, the first of five pictures from the famous Cook Collection of which the

*The present record is £2,310,000 paid at Christies in 1970 for Velasquez's portrait, *Juan de Pareja*.

Rembrandt was the most important. Mr Simon made nearly all his bids by calling out 'Five hundred' (500 guineas), thus drawing attention to himself and to the fact that he was not familiar with the normal procedure in British salerooms. When the bidding has passed 20,000 guineas it is usual for the auctioneer to raise the bidding by at least 1,000 guineas at a time, but Mr Simon went on with his calls of 'Five hundred' until even the 30,000-guineas mark was left behind. Even so he failed to get the picture, which went to Colnaghi at 38,000 guineas (£39,900). In view of his subsequent statement that he wanted to avoid publicity until the Rembrandt was cleared for export to America, his behaviour was extremely foolish. The newspapermen were immediately interested in him and were watching him closely when the Rembrandt came up four lots later.

'Lot 105. One hundred thousand guineas offered,' said the auctioneer, Christie's chairman Mr I O 'Peter' Chance. The bidding leapt up, first in twenty-thousands then fifty-thousands and reached half-a-million in less than thirty seconds. Then Mr Simon, who had been bidding openly by raising a finger and nodding his head, called out excitedly, 'Six hundred thousand!' and the auctioneer came straight back with, 'And fifty'. At that stage there were still at least four prospective buyers in the running. Dealer Geoffrey Agnew was sitting a few rows behind Mr Simon and as the American forced the pace he countered all his bids with discreet, almost imperceptible nods. But his interest ended at 700,000 guineas. Mr Simon indicated one more bid, 720,000 guineas, and then he remembered belatedly that he wanted to remain anonymous. So, when a counterbid of 740,000 guineas came from the Duke of Beaufort's heir, David Somerset, acting for his firm, Marlborough Fine Art, Mr Simon sat tight and said nothing (someone later affirmed that he was winking at the auctioneer but this was never confirmed.)

For long seconds the auctioneer looked meaningful looks at Mr Simon and Mr Simon looked meaningful looks back at him, but neither got the other's meaning. 'Any more? More? Bidding?' asked Mr Chance, who was clearly reluctant to knock the picture down. 'It's against you,' he said leaning perilously far over the edge of his rostrum towards Mr Simon. When no reply came from the American the auctioneer surveyed the rest of the room, repeated, 'Seven hundred and forty thousand guineas' and 'Any more?' again and again, then rapped his little gavel and announced, 'Marlborough Fine Art'.

Immediately there was pandemonium. Spontaneous applause clashed with cries of anguish from Mr Simon. 'I am still bidding!' The smile of triumph died on Mr Chance's face. Above the noise he called down to the American, 'I said quite clearly it was against you.' And of course we all knew that he had. But Mr Simon was jumping mad. 'You got my message, Mr Chance,' he shouted back. 'You had definite instructions what to watch for.' Mr Chance looked baffled and shrugged his shoulders. 'All right,' said Mr Simon pulling a piece of paper out of his pocket, 'I will read what it says here.' In fact he first gave the paper to Mr Tooth to read out but when the dealer was unable to make himself heard he took it back and read it himself at the top of his voice. It soon became clear that it was a letter from Christie's outlining a secret bidding arrangement that Mr Simon was to use when bidding for the Rembrandt. It said:

> When Mr Simon is sitting down he is bidding. If he bids openly he is also bidding. When he stands up he has stopped bidding. If he sits down again he is not bidding unless he raises

his finger. Having raised his finger he is bidding until he stands up again.

Confronted with the letter Mr Chance decided that the bidding must be resumed where it had left off. Mr Somerset made a mild protest but was overruled. There was only one more bid – the American's 760,000 guineas. As he knocked the picture down for the second time, the auctioneer announced in a loud, clear voice, 'The Norton Simon Foundation'. Simon's complicated plan to keep his identity secret had failed and, in doing so, had soured Christie's moment of triumph over Sotheby's from whom they had snatched not only the record for the highest priced picture but also that for the biggest total turnover at a single sale in Britain, £1,186,279*.

Some people blamed Mr Simon, others thought it was Christie's own fault for accepting such an absurdly involved bidding code. But for the Press the story could scarcely have been better. It had everything – big money, a row, mystery – everything except sex (and some reporters even managed to hint at that by reminding their readers that Lady Cook, who sold the Rembrandt, was the seventh wife of Sir Francis Cook). There was so much to write about that many other interesting aspects of the sale were completely ignored and a much crazier example of secret bidding carried out in the reporters' midst went unreported (except by me).

A few minutes before the Rembrandt came up, one of the directors of Agnew's left his seat in the body of the room, joined the photographers and reporters near the auctioneer's rostrum and began to bid for Lot 101A, a *Nativity,* only $5\frac{3}{4}$ ins by $3\frac{3}{4}$ ins, by Fra Bartolommeo. To the majority of people in the

*The present record is £3,638,825 paid at Christie's in June 1971 for twenty-seven Old Masters, one of which, Titian's *The Death of Actæon,* realised £1,680,000.

saleroom it must have appeared that he was a very coy fellow consulting his own feet for advice between each bid. Only those near him realised that he was relaying bids from a young man who had come into the room by the back door and was now sitting at his feet giving him instructions. At 20,000 guineas the young man gave up and left by the back door shrouded in an air of mystery and a drab raincoat. The picture was bought in at 22,000 guineas and Agnew's man returned to his seat.

The great variety of ways of bidding would make an interesting subject for a student of psychology. Even the way in which a man or woman waves a catalogue is revealing, not only of character but also of circumstance. I once commented to an auctioneer on the way in which a Continental dealer flicked his catalogue in just the same couldn't-care-less fashion whether he was bidding in fivers or five-thousands. 'That's because it wasn't his own money,' said the auctioneer. 'He was working on commission.' But no one ever explained to me why a certain Parisian dealer, a woman, made her bids by giving the auctioneer a succession of unsubtle winks.

Still, a wink is as good as a nod, and, from the auctioneer's point of view, the clearer it is, the better. In spite of this, most regular frequenters of the salerooms prefer to bid unobtrusively, even furtively; for the spirit of Joseph Duveen (who would often outbid his rivals on principle, whether he wanted a picture or not) is not completely dead. Auctioneers flourish on the rivalry of the dealers and it is therefore to a dealer's advantage if he can keep his intentions to himself. Sometimes he will go to great lengths to achieve this. He may, for example, bid up to a certain point and then make a show of dropping out whereas, in fact, the clerk or someone unknown to his rivals has taken over from him. The mere fact that a leading dealer – an Agnew, a Colnaghi, a Knoedler, or a Wildenstein, perhaps – is seen to be bidding for a particular picture is often equivalent to publishing a free valuation of the picture and in these days, when more 'and more private collectors are buying direct from the salerooms, this can mean a serious loss to a dealer. A collector does not have to be very clever to work out that, dealers' profit ratios being what they are, he will probably get a picture he wants much more cheaply by outbidding a dealer at an auction than he will ever be able to get it at a later date. This procedure is not, however, recommended to beginners for, as I have shown elsewhere, it can be very hazardous. It is certainly not for you yet, so let us go back to your sale, which is now getting towards its end.

All the most important lots have gone, many of the prices have run into four figures, one or two have made over £10,000 and the fact that your picture is in such a good sale seems to augur well. You are perhaps a little worried that many people, including some of the dealers, have already left but your common sense tells you that the number of prospective buyers for any particular picture must always be very few. You need only two keen, would-be buyers. Even if there is only one you may get your reserve price. You keep your fingers crossed as the auctioneer says, 'Lot so-and-so. Fifty pounds anybody?' Only fifty pounds? What is he doing, trying to give it away? 'Fifty pounds?' You feel panicky. Doesn't anybody want it even at fifty pounds? You feel desperate enough to start the bidding yourself. But then the auctioneer, whose impassivity you had previously admired but now find maddening, says, 'Fifty pounds I'm bid.' He pauses for a moment. 'Eighty . . . One hundred . . . One twenty . . . One fifty . . . One eighty.' Another pause. He repeats, 'One eighty,' and looks round the room. 'Two hundred . . . And fifty . . .' (a bigger jump there, but no one seems to notice) . . . Three hundred, three-fifty, four hundred. Again he searches the room. If only you had accepted the reserve price the young man suggested the picture would be sold by now, you think. The idea of getting the picture back unsold after all this is unbearable.

'Are you bidding, madam?' says the auctioneer to a woman in the tenth row. 'Oh no', she says. She was only shading her eyes with her catalogue! Please let *someone* bid, you say to yourself. And the auctioneer says, 'Four hundred and fifty, Five hundred.' You are home! But are you? Can it be a Finkelbaum or Hogginbotham bid? No, it can't, unless the auctioneer has made a mistake. 'Five hundred and fifty . . . Five hundred and fifty pounds then . . .' Now you know it is sold. Relief is followed immediately by wild hopes. Perhaps it will go much higher. A thousand even? 'Five hundred and fifty pounds,' says the auctioneer yet again and you see him raise the little ivory hammer-head in his left hand. But just as he raps it down one of the dealers in the front row raises his catalogue. Quickly the auctioneer retrieves the situation. 'With the hammer', he says. 'I'm sorry. Six hundred pounds. It's six hundred against you, sir,' The bidder who thought he had been successful at £550 comes back equally quickly with another bid. 'Six hundred and fifty,' says the auctioneer to the front-row dealer who shakes his head. And that is it. The auctioneer repeats, 'Six hundred and fifty,' taps his hammer and says a name. You didn't catch the name. But you can be sure it wasn't Finkelbaum or Hogginbotham.

The rest of the sale holds no interest for you. You are wondering whether it was all worth the strain. The price is, as they said 'between six and eight hundred'. When they have deducted their 12½ per cent commission (it would have been fifteen per cent if your picture had fetched £500 or less, and ten per cent if it had gone over £10,000) and Value Added Tax on that commission and a small charge for insurance you will get a little less than £560. Now you begin to think that if only you could have taken it direct to the dealer who bought it, or even to that one in the front row, you would have got more. But don't you believe it. The rivalry of the saleroom usually obliges the dealer to pay a higher price there than he would to a private vendor, especially an inexperienced private vendor. Be content. You did very well for a beginner. And if one day when you are in St James's you see what appears to be a newly painted version of your picture in a dealer's window don't be surprised (it is amazing what cleaning can do). Go in and ask how much it is. Then try to keep your temper. A hundred per cent mark up is nothing in the art game.

10

Dealers, Geese and Golden Eggs

Inevitably one had to start thinking of oneself more as a capital broker than as the purveyor of luxury goods one used to be in the past.

SIR GEOFFREY AGNEW,*

The fact that you sold your flowerpiece in the saleroom was significant. Not so long ago you would almost certainly have taken it to a dealer. The modern fashion among private individuals to sell at auction is an even bigger thorn in the sides of the dealers than the growing habit of collectors to buy for themselves in the salerooms. It hurts their pride. Their roles as the kings of the business have been largely usurped by the auctioneers upon whom they are now much more dependent than ever before. In the old days a nobleman who wished to raise a few thousand pounds on the family heirlooms, for example, would almost invariably have approached one of the great dealers in confidence. Today he not only goes to Sotheby's or Christie's but also permits his name to be published in the

*Quoted by John Pearson in *Sunday Times* Colour Supplement 17 March 1963.

sale catalogue and hence in the Press. The old, gentlemanly deal, in which the seller was satisfied with a reasonable price that made it possible for the dealer to sell at a reasonable price and so make another of his clients happy, is replaced by a cut-throat duel in the saleroom. The effects of this are reflected in two remarks made by one of the directors of Agnew's. 'My family has lived for 150 years largely by selling pictures to one generation and buying them back from the next,' he said. And then, a few sentences later, 'The trouble today is not to sell the finest pictures but to find them in the first place'.*

But although the private owner of Old Masters who sells at auction has created a big headache for the big dealers (the smaller dealers prefer the 'free-for-all') the private buyer of Old Masters in the saleroom is too rare a bird to cause him much trouble. Very few of the wealthy collectors of Old Masters who might seriously menace the big dealers in the saleroom have the knowledge to do so. They can, if they wish, make use of the advice of the auctioneers' 'experts' but they do so at their own risk. Whereas a reputable dealer will give a guarantee of authenticity, the auctioneers, as we saw in Chapter Five, disclaim all responsibility for 'errors of description, or for the genuineness or authenticity of any lot or for any fault or defect'. So the collector who is spending thousands of pounds on an Old Master, may still prefer to spend a few more thousands for the benefit of the dealer's expert knowledge and the obligation that his reputation imposes upon him to guarantee what he sells.

When we come to Impressionist and Modern pictures, however, things are very different because the problem of authentication is not nearly so great. During the past ten years

*Quoted by John Pearson *op cit.*

184

private buyers in the saleroom have spoiled the Impressionist market from the dealer's point of view by forcing the prices so high that there is much less margin left for the dealer's profit. Private buyers had been greatly encouraged to bid for themselves when, in 1962, Sotheby's introduced a new condition, relating to 'Impressionist and Modern' and 'Modern British' picture sales which gave them the authority to rescind the sale of any lot of which it was shown, within three weeks, that there was 'serious doubt as to authenticity'. But we need shed no tears over the dealers. The general increase of business in their trade more than compensates for any pirate raids the collector may make on what was once almost exclusively their territory. You have only to count up the number of prosperous commercial galleries in London to see that business is booming as never before.

In 1974 there were more than 200 (the number has doubled in ten years) commercial art galleries in London, the majority of them within the square mile bounded by Oxford Street, Regent Street, Park Lane, and King Street, St James's. Some have been there a hundred years or more; one, at least, is likely to have opened only last month. For various reasons dealers in most trades have always tended to congregate in a particular district. And the reason for this concentration is obvious. Art is expensive and this is where the money is. Though Mayfair is no longer predominantly a residential area for the rich it is still the place where they spend their money, just as it was when Agnews moved into their converted coach-house in Bond Street more than a hundred years ago, just as it was in 1843 when Christie's moved into their King Street premises. Although in recent years a number of galleries have been successfully established outside this area it remains the heart of the art market.

But inside this heart revolutionary changes have taken place since the war.

Until then, in spite of the swashbuckling activities of Duveen, the trade went on in much the same quiet way as it had for a century or two, following the pattern set by the demand of more or less serious art collectors for a supply of more or less important Old Masters. But after the last war, as inflation created large numbers of collectors whose primary interest in art was its relative safety as an investment, two major changes developed. First, as the run on good Old Masters revealed that supplies were getting very low and that it was not enough simply to charge the earth for those that remained, new supplies, or rather supplies of something new, had to be found. The Impressionists and Post-Impressionists were the obvious answer, and after them the masters of the Ecole de Paris and even a few British home-grown artists. The second change (it may have been first – the two were related chicken-and-egg-wise) came about when the possiblities of the art trade began to attract the attention of certain gentlemen whose knowledge of art may have been limited but who, perhaps because of this, perceived that there was no reason why it should not be marketed by the same modern, high-pressure sales methods that were proving so successful in less hallowed fields of commerce.

The effect on the old-style dealers was at first traumatic, but for most it turned out later to be therapeutic, a shock treatment from which they emerged with renewed vigour to battle with the newcomers. A few of the Old Master dealers made token protests at being turned into investment brokers but soon allowed their wounded pride to be assuaged by the increased profits that accrued. For every one of the old brigade who succumbed there were half a dozen newcomers to take his place, most of them fired by the prospect of fat profits made all the more attractive for having been wrung from 'culture'. Among the scores of men and women who have begun art dealing and/or have opened galleries in London in the years since the war are a typewriter-salesman, a wholesaler of zip fasteners, a chemist, a cotton manufacturer, a 'laundrette' proprietor, a tympanist, an archaeologist, an orchestral conductor, a racing journalist, a professional Quaker, the heir to a cooking-fats fortune, a City financier's son, an ex-colonel of the Guards, a Member of Parliament, an economist, a dairy-farmer, an actor and two ladies' hairdressers. By no means everyone who attempted to break in stayed in. Many learned the hard way that there is much more to successful art dealing than opening up shop in Bond Street, or its environs and waiting for rich Americans from Claridges or the Westbury to drop in and buy. But for some there was spectacular financial success, none more spectacular than that of Frank Lloyd and Harry Fischer, two Austrian refugees whose impact on the art trade has been felt far beyond Bond Street, in Europe and America.

Although both came from Vienna, where Fischer was a bookseller and Lloyd owned a string of petrol service-stations, they met for the first time during the war while serving in that curious cosmopolitan section of the British Army, the Pioneer Corps. The story goes that while still in khaki they agreed that after the war they would, in partnership, make themselves the biggest art merchants in Europe. Whether the story is true or not is now a purely academic question. The fact is that Marlborough Fine Art, the firm they started in Bond Street in 1946, became the biggest art business in the world. It is probably still the biggest, even though Messrs Fischer and Lloyd parted company in 1972 and some of their major artists went with

Fischer to his new company, Fischer Fine Arts. Today, the two former partners bid furiously against each other in the salerooms – and against several of their former employees, casualties of the split, each of whom, armed with Marlborough know-how and Marlborough's list of clients, is dealing very successfully on his own account.

It is unlikely that the success of Marlborough Fine Art could be repeated again in our time (although the inflationary circumstances that did much to make it possible are still with us). But there are still plenty of opportunities for the enterprising to make a pile, or at any rate a living, the art way. It is no longer necessary to have a gallery in the West End of London. It is not necessary to have a gallery anywhere. One of London's richest dealers has only a small office and a store-room. Others, like the remarkable Mr Julius Weitzner, work successfully without leaving their homes except to go to sales. Several dealers sell almost entirely by post; several more ship everything they buy direct to the United States, or to Japan.

To be a dealer, then, all one has to do is to know where and what to buy and where and for how much it can be sold. This may mean, as it does for one dealer I know, an elaborate card index of scores of sources of supply and thousands of customers each of whom has a special interest – one wants topographical drawings of the county he was born in; another collects paintings by artists whose name is the same as his own; a third wants prints of anything to do with railways; and so on. To another dealer, who knows from long experience the cheapest sort of quality in pictures that the big auctioneers will accept for sale, it simply means buying works of that quality at the smaller auction houses and taking them along to Sotheby's or Christie's where almost invariably they will fetch appreciably more than he has paid for them. To a third, who may know very little about painting but works on the reasonable assumption that virtually everything sold at Sotheby's or Christie's must have some value, it means attending every picture sale in those auction-rooms, being ready to snap up anything that is going for a few pounds and, later, selling them to other dealers or putting them back in the saleroom again. His motto is 'There is at least one bargain in every sale.' And he is right.

The process of 'selling pictures to one generation and buying them back from the next', by which Agnew's achieved prosperity has a parallel today. As any regular frequenter of the auction-rooms and art-galleries can see the same sort of thing is happening all the time on a lower level and at a speeded-up rate. A considerable proportion of pictures at any one time is circulating like a chain letter among dealers, private buyer-speculators, and salerooms. In most cases everyone concerned makes a profit but one cannot help feeling that, as with chain letters, there is a catch somewhere. Someone at the end of the line, it seems, must lose. But this is not necessarily true. In recent times art prices generally have risen so rapidly and consistently that however high a price a buyer has paid for a work by an artist with a market rating he has had to wait only a year or two to be able to sell at a profit – even to the dealer from whom he bought it in the first place. Indeed, the waiting time has become progressively shorter and shorter over the years as prices have gone higher and higher.

I once upset a wealthy collector by remarking tactlessly that a Post-Impressionist picture he had just bought from a dealer for £25,000 had been bought by the dealer in the saleroom only a few months earlier for £16,000. He was livid. He had no idea the dealers made so much profit. It was criminal, he said, and threatened to tell the dealer what he thought of him, etc. The fact that he had been 'cheated' put him off the picture so much that after eighteen months he sold it in the saleroom. It fetched £32,000. So far as I am aware he did not then feel that he must share his profit with the dealer. But he does now think the dealer is a wonderful chap and always buys from him.

In this case the dealer's profit, although it may seem high, was soon seen to have been fully justified. He had bought cheaply and, even after he had added more than fifty per cent profit, the price was still reasonable. Generally, if a dealer buys at a bargain price he will, for a good customer, fix his selling price accordingly. In other cases he will probably calculate his profit broadly in accordance with a descending scale of percentages that begins at a hundred per cent, or more, on items for which he has paid up to, say, £500, falls to fifty per cent on items that cost him £10,000, and to twenty-five per cent on £50,000. In this way the dealers have established a general price range whose relation to saleroom prices should be understood by the collector-investor who is thinking primarily of a quick profit.

Understandably, most dealers are reluctant to let their clients know what they themselves have paid for the pictures they sell but in many cases their secrets are no secrets. A surprisingly large proportion of the pictures sold by London dealers are bought in the principal London salerooms, each of which issues price lists after every sale. Very often, therefore, the prospective buyer of a picture can discover without much trouble what profit the dealer is making. For the big-time dealer there would seem to be an additional problem in that many of his purchases are reported in the Press, but according to several I have talked with this is not so. Press publicity of this sort can be of tremendous value in drawing the attention of prospective buyers, especially public galleries in this country and abroad, to the availability of an important picture. Because of the way in which most great public galleries are controlled, purchasing is generally done by committees. This means that they rarely buy direct from the salerooms but must wait until a picture is in the hands of a dealer so that they can borrow it and sit on it in committee until agreement is reached. From the taxpayer's or ratepayer's point of view this is a crazy way of going on, as was shown in November 1973 when seven sketchbooks of the watercolourist, John Robert Cozens (1752-97) came up for sale at Sotheby's. Each sketchbook was to be sold as a separate lot, and because of the probability that they would be bought by dealers and broken up for sale Sotheby's illustrated every sketch in their catalogue as a permanent record of the books in their entirety. But at the sale it was made known that the owner, the Duke of Hamilton and Brandon, had decided that the seven sketchbooks should be sold as one lot, and they went for £120,000 to the Bond Street dealer, Leger, with the Bond Street dealer, Agnew as underbidder at £110,000. After the event it was made known that Agnew had been bidding on behalf of the British Museum and that the Duke had asked for the books to be sold together so as to make it easier for the Museum to acquire them for the nation. Had the British Museum been represented in the saleroom by a known member of its staff, it is unlikely that any dealer would have pushed the price up to anything like £120,000. Hard on the poor Duke? Not really, for the sum the sketchbooks fetched was twice as much as Sotheby's had told him to expect.

In justification of the big profit made on a high-priced picture it should be remembered that often a very risky gamble

191

is involved, that in many cases it may mean that a large capital sum is tied up for a long period before a buyer is found, that during that period the value of the picture at auction will probably have risen automatically, and that the business of finding the buyer may itself be costly.

But, to come down to earth, let me recall the remarkable price-histories of a few humbler pictures that I observed going the rounds in the sixties. The first concerns one of those very fly characters known as 'knockers' whom we met in Chapter Six – that is the small-time dealers, usually, as in this case, furniture or antique dealers, who buy their stock by calling at private houses and persuading unsuspecting housewives to part with anything saleable. (A rather more respectable form of knocking is practised by even the highest class of dealers and auctioneers. Few of them would hesitate to pull strings to get introductions to owners of Old Masters rumoured to be hard-up and thinking of selling – Joe Duveen was the King of such knockers – and those more interested in Modern pictures are not above importuning the widows and families of famous modern artists). Our particular knocker bought a watercolour for £2 and sold it to another of his fraternity for £5. This second knocker put it into a minor London saleroom where it was sold for £14. The buyer, a small-time picture-dealer, sold it before he had left the saleroom to a collector-speculator for £25. This gentleman took it to Sotheby's where, a few months later, it was bought by a West-End dealer for £55. The dealer put it in his annual Christmas-present show at £120 and sold it to a collector who, so far as I am aware, still has it. The watercolour is by Edward Lear, whose prices have risen so much since this happened in 1963 that its saleroom value today, ten years later would be about £400.

I was in at the beginning of my second history, which began in late 1964 and is still progressing. I walked into a minor London saleroom just as what appeared, at ten yards distance, to be a very attractive little landscape was being knocked down at £14. Having boobed once or twice in the past by buying attractive-looking pictures that I had not examined in advance, I resisted the temptation to bid, but after the sale I asked the buyer, a suburban dealer, if I might see it. The little picture had been catalogued as 'Ibbetson' and we both agreed that it could be by that artist.* I offered to buy it on the spot at four times the price he had paid but the dealer wanted to 'do some work on it first'. This work, I learned subsequently, consisted primarily in taking the picture to one of the biggest Old Master dealers in Bond Street, asking his opinion, and offering it for sale. The big man's opinion was that it was not by Ibbetson but that it was worth £70. The little man sold. Imagine his surprise then when I told him, a few weeks later, that 'his' picture was in the Christmas exhibition of an off-Bond-Street dealer (nothing to do with the big man) and priced at £320. And that was not all. In June 1965 I saw the picture in a Knightsbridge antique shop and asked the price. 'Four hundred and twenty guineas,' replied the antique-dealer. By 1973, when a superb watercolour by Ibbetson *Skating on the Serpentine* fetched £18,900 at Christies, that little oil must have been worth well over £1000.

The third history concerns a 'runner' – a man who acts as an agent to other dealers, keeping his eyes and ears open for anything that may interest them, while all the time nursing the hope that he will one day be able to set up as a dealer himself. This runner bought an Old Master drawing so cheaply at a

*Julius Caesar Ibbetson, 1759-1817.

country sale that he decided to keep it to himself. He put it into a London sale where it made £40 – nearly eight times as much as he had paid for it. The buyer, a small-time dealer, sold it to one of the West End Dealers whom the runner often helped, for £100. But that was not the end. In the meantime the runner had described the drawing to an American dealer who was very interested and asked to see it. Without mentioning that it was no longer his the runner promised to bring it to him. He went to the West End dealer, who was now offering the drawing at £400, and said that he thought he could sell it for him. The dealer let him have it and promised him ten per cent commission if he made a sale. The American was very impressed by the drawing and asked how much it was. The runner quickly added another hundred to the price – and got it! It is probably only a matter of time before the drawing comes back to the London saleroom to be sold as part of an important collection of Old Master drawings and fetches thousands of pounds.

Things of this sort are happening all the time. There is probably some such story behind a large proportion of all the pictures, especially the older ones, that come on to the market. But not all of them are quite so happy for all concerned. There is the sad tale of the young art reporter who, when hard up, sold a gouache, given to him by an artist whose work he had praised, to a friend for £20. When the artist suddenly became successful the young man cunningly bought back the gouache for £25 and sold it to a dealer for £80. The dealer hung it in his gallery, priced at £150. The reporter was very angry at having been 'done'. A little later he was even angrier when he saw a similar gouache in another gallery marked £320 on the back. Then he had the bright idea of buying back his gouache from the first dealer (who generously let him have it for £120)

194

and offering it to the second dealer for £220. But the second dealer laughed and showed him his own gouache which, he said, he would gladly sell for £90. The '£320' on the back, he explained, was the price of the picture that had been in the frame before the gouache. Exit young art reporter crestfallen.

In my experience it is usually the get-rich-quick, fly-by-night dealers who try to make exorbitant profits that have no fair relation to a picture's present or potential value. The wise dealer (and most of the well-established ones are very wise in this respect) knows just how far he can go without frightening a client away. Those dealers who run galleries in which they show the work of living artists explain that much of the money they make on *dealing* goes to subsidise exhibitions of work by new artists. Although this may be little consolation to the man who pays £40,000 for a £30,000 picture there is in most cases a measure of truth in the explanation. Few dealers in the West End of London could survive on the proceeds of the one-man shows by living artists that they hold. Many regard them simply as 'window-dressing'. The really profitable business is done behind the scenes usually by selling the work of dead artists. Until Marlborough Fine Art's high-powered promotion of artists like Moore, Sutherland, Bacon, and Ben Nicholson, showed the way to make British art pay, most dealers had no alternative but to regard exhibitions of work by British artists as acts of altruism. But because Marlborough made a handful of British artists pay in a big way this did not mean that the whole picture was changed. The number of serious British artists (that is artists who should be taken seriously) whose one-man shows are financially worthwhile for their dealers still cannot be more than a few dozen. Those outside the Marlborough and Fischer stables who make big money can be numbered on the toes of a one legged man.

Generally, when an artist has a one-man show, the dealer's share is $33\frac{1}{3}$ per cent of the proceeds of all sales. In some cases it is as high as fifty per cent. The considerable cost of framing has to be met by the artist but the dealer usually pays for the catalogues and may provide an opening-night party. When he gives an unknown artist an exhibition the dealer takes a gamble that justifies the high rate of commission. But there is no reduction in the rate of commission if the artist proves to be a big success. The $33\frac{1}{3}$ per cent will continue to be exacted from his sales at all subsequent exhibitions. Thus the dealer's initial gamble can prove to be usefully profitable and he may decide it is to his advantage to bind the artist to him by a contract, on the principle that, as one dealer put it, it is silly to buy golden eggs when you can buy the goose that lays them.

Such contracts may carry with them an agreement by which the dealer pays a regular monthly 'salary' to the artist which is offset against his sales. Although arrangements of this sort have existed in France since the beginning of the century they were virtually unknown in Britain until after the last war. First to start giving contracts in London were three dealers who had learned the trade in Paris, Charles and Peter Gimpel, of Gimpel Fils, and Erica Brausen, of the Hanover Gallery. But it was not until about 1960, when Marlborough Fine Art moved into the field, that the practice began to become fairly widespread.

At that time Marlborough's high-powered, and sometimes high-handed, activities were causing some envy and ill-feeling among older established dealers. It was particularly galling for those who, after having nursed certain British artists to the point where they were beginning to yield handsome returns,

found that those artists were succumbing to the lure of contracts from Marlborough that would provide them with
handsome and regular incomes, relieve them of such mundane
worries as income tax problems and guarantee them exhibitions
in London's most up-to-date gallery. But there was also a
sneaking admiration for Marlborough's enterprise and this
showed itself in ways that were all, to some extent, beneficial to
the artists. Many dealers began to spruce up their galleries and
give them a new look and new lighting. Ideas among the
dealers about the monetary value of contemporary British art
changed – to the advantage of the artists and dealers and, in the
long run, of the collectors. Following Marlborough's example,
too, those dealers who were agents for British artists showed
increased support for their artists in the salerooms, bidding for
any of their works that came up for auction to ensure that their
prices were maintained. In nearly all the activities of dealers in
modern paintings Marlborough set the pace.

Most criticism of the contract system is based on the
romantic, *vie de Bohème* fallacy that artists do their best work
when they are starving and that comfort and security are
inimical to inspiration. But it is also said that the system gives
the dealer too much power over the artist, and that the artist is
no longer his own master and is told not only when, where,
and for how much his work shall be sold but also what sort of
pictures he must paint, and in this there is certainly some truth.
In the old days an artist had a one-man show when he had
enough good work ready. Now, if he is a 'tied' artist, he is
likely to be working always with an exhibition date hanging
over him. And he is likely to be working with the primary
object of selling rather than creating. If, in doing this, he is
inclined to play safe and repeat the sort of things with which

he has been successful in the past, he may well be encouraged to do so by his dealer.

Whether a contract is a good thing depends very much on the temperament of the artist. Some artists find no difficulty at all in fulfilling themselves and the terms of the contract. Others are temperamentally unsuited to working to deadlines and are unable to say 'no' to anything their dealers suggest. I have known one of Britain's most distinguished painters so pressed for time that, as he confessed to me, he had to paint half the pictures for his biennial one-man show in a month (and that was how the exhibition looked). And I have seen what looked suspiciously like potboiler drawings served up, to meet a demand, by one of our greatest sculptors.

But in spite of its dangers (and in the case of the young artist prematurely signed up and pressure-promoted by a high-powered dealer they can be very great) I think that the contract system has done more good than harm and I would like to see it spread. It is obvious, however, that it must always be limited to a very small proportion of working artists, for no dealer will give a contract to an artist unless he is fairly sure that he will one day pay his way, and the number of artists that even today's booming art market can or will support to the tune of even £3,000 a year is comparatively few.

I have said that to be a dealer all one has to know is where and what to buy and where and for how much to sell it, but if I make it sound easy that is a mistake, a mistake that many would-be dealers have made. As I have shown again and again the field is vast and is thick with booby-traps. For this reason most dealers specialise in a particular part of the field and may know surprisingly little about the other parts. A few years ago writer-chef-comedian, and now Member of Parliament, Clement

Freud decided to test whether London's top art-dealers were frank, helpful, knowledgeable. Writing of his experiences, in *The Queen* magazine, he came to the conclusion that 'the answers loosely would appear to be yes, yes, no'.

His test consisted of hawking three nondescript little pictures and a '£4,000' Renoir drawing signed 'AR' round a number of galleries and asking for any offers. He wore a day's growth of beard and gave a false name. At Spink's, a firm that specialised in antiquities and coins, the Renoir was, understandably perhaps, not even recognised as a Renoir. The same thing happened at Wildenstein's where, if the bosses were at lunch, even the office boy might reasonably have been expected to know a Renoir. Agnew's, who were then almost exclusively Old Master men, thought it was most likely by Renoir but were not interested enough to make an offer. At Marlborough Fine Art two young men argued about it, one rejecting the idea that it was by Renoir, the other suggesting it might be a Renoir forgery. Only Tooth's representative thought it might be worth a lot of money* and advised taking it to a Renoir expert for authentication.

As a test of dealers' knowledge it was hardly fair since it would appear that only at Spink's and Tooth's was the opinion given by a senior member of the firm. It might equally well have been said to illustrate the honesty of dealers, not only because they gave their opinions so frankly, but because even where the Renoir was recognised no attempt was made to take advantage of Freud's feigned anxiety to raise money on it. One aspect of the account that might justly have caused some concern, however, was that all the dealers appear to have accepted

*Not long afterwards the drawing came up for sale at Sotheby's – and was knocked down at £1,800.

without suspicion Freud's story that he had found the pictures in the attic of a house he had just bought. Yet a few years earlier the Renoir had been shown at the O'Hana Gallery and had been bought there by a well-known collector who had lent it to Freud for his experiment. So much for the oft-quoted theory that such works are so well recorded that it would be impossible for a thief to sell them.

The really successful dealer is a man who combines something of the psychologist, the stockbroker, the impressario, the public relations man, and the detective, with a touch of aesthetic sensibility and some knowledge of artists' methods of working. He has insight into the collector's mentality; the ability to anticipate price trends and the power to create them; a sense of showmanship in presenting his wares and an understanding of the value of publicity; a nose for what is good and for what is false; enough knowledge of techniques and art history to be one jump ahead of most of his clients and to be able to talk intelligently to the others; and such enthusiasm for what he is selling, whether it is by an Old Master, a very minor Impressionist, or the latest young unknown in his stable, that his clients feel he is doing them a favour. An instinctive flair for the game and the experience that comes from years of handling pictures will be far more valuable to him than any amount of book-learning. Duveen, who in Behrman's words 'seldom read anything', was interested in art books only when they confirmed his own opinions. When he was asked, in the course of one of his many lawsuits, if he knew Ruskin's *Stones of Venice*, he replied that 'he had heard of the picture but never actually seen it.' And when his *gaffe* was pointed out to him afterwards he just laughed. He could afford to. When he died, in 1939, he left the best part of a million pounds.

Today when the art game has become a free-for-all, there are many newcomers who have few of these attributes and yet contrive to make a lot of money out of dealing. As in so many fields today they lack not only knowledge, experience, and sensibility but also integrity. They take advantage of the greed of people even more ignorant than themselves to make exorbitant profits from things that, in any but a wildly inflationary period such as the present, would be (and, I hope, will again be) considered worthless.

11

Critics and
Hypocritics

Critics are sheepborn, sheepsuckled by a schoolmarm and half asheep when faced with a work of art. The difference between artist and critic is this: the artist creates, the critic bleats.

KURT SCHWITTERS

My own instinct tells me that the didactic critic who practises a 'scientific' formal method of criticism refuses to engage in the expression of his feelings only because that critic himself has a deep hatred for the act of creation, for the artist's preoccupation with creation. To hide this hatred he builds his facade of higher learning. That is why I call it hypocriticism. Only passionate criticism is honest criticism.

BARNETT NEWMAN

'Primarily a critic is a signpost,' wrote Clive Bell way back in 1919. 'He points to a work of art and says – "Stop! Look!" To do that he must have the sensibility that distinguishes works of art from rubbish . . .' Bell's extraordinary self-assurance is still impressive, but, unlike the critic of today, he was never put to the ultimate test of a confrontation with a heap of rubbish exhibited in a major art exhibition held in a major art-gallery subsidised by the British Government. He might (although it is very doubtful) have just heard of Kurt Schwitters and the use that artist was making of bits of rubbish in his *Merz* pictures. But that was rubbish 'transformed by selection and rearrangement made by an artist.' He had certainly never seen an art-gallery filled from floor to ceiling from a city's dustcarts or been asked to review an 'important international exhibition' (see Chapter Twelve) which included a compost-heap, an ash-heap, and a pile of dead leaves among the 'works' on show.

What would he have said if he had? Would he have seen only rubbish in such things and have had the courage to say so? Or would he, like most critics of today, have been afraid of being seen to be out of step, not only with the new art but also with the new criticism. For nowadays art criticism has become as tricky a business as the new art itself. Indeed, the art criticism is the trickier. As art became simpler, or rather, as artists strove for greater and greater simplification, art criticism became more and more abtruse. Because the artist had reduced his own invention to a minimum, the critic was obliged (if he was to keep his job) to resort to his own powers of invention, such as they were, to fill his column. So, minimalist art (see Chapter Twelve) produced maximalist critics. Seeing little or nothing that they could write about with passion or dared to write about with honesty, they 'invented words', as the gargantuan collector, Joe Hirshhorn put it. And in case you do not know what he meant, here are a couple of examples:

> His concern with orthogonals and modular measure dominated post-and-lintel architecture during centuries of anthro-

pomorphic sculpture. LeWitt's structures have always been related to their architectural contexts – if only by having primary measurements determined by the ability to pass through the average door. To me, the visual activity demanded by LeWitt's work has always been less like that of Rembrandt or Brancusi (which themselves fuse direct information of 'signs' into artistically interpreted 'symbols') than that of 'reading' directly informative 'signs' in a temporary additive sequence without any artistically provided interpretational fusion. Of course, LeWitt limits the meaningful information of what is 'read' to itself as visually perceived phenomena; his absolutely non-utilitarian 'signs' demand reception from a free, active, and wide-ranging thoughtfulness for further significance.

Or:

Balanci contributes a synthetic-dimension. He takes hold of space, makes an abstract organisation of it, renders it dynamic by the effective truth of reality accepted photographically, as well as by the aberrant power of the depersonalisation of the already real; by these means Balanci imposes his entirely recomposed image – clean, dynamic, perturbing, and yet serene in its latent reality. As from now, Balanci has assumed the responsibility for the transformation of contemporary artistic ambitions.

The part played by critics in the breakdown of standards in the art of the last decade cannot be overstated. Most, even most of the more intelligent ones, acted as cheer-leaders, standing on the sidelines, egging on the perpetrators of every ridiculous excess, encouraging the cult of the 'new for new's sake'. Everything, however inane, was accepted at the artist's own (often tongue-in-cheek) valuation and treated with a respect it rarely deserved. However stupid an artist's work, however deliberately sensational, however gimmicky, there was always a critic to praise and boost it. And if that critic was an 'influential' one, then most of the others would go along with him like Schwitters's sheep. Search through back numbers of the art journals and you will be lucky to find a single word of reproof for an artist or an exhibition. Nor are you likely to find a single witty or amusing line at the expense of the artist or the exhibition. It was all deadly earnest, pompous and dull.

There were probably many reasons for this state of affairs. One of them was the pressure, real or imaginary, exerted by the journal's advertisers, most of whom were the dealers who put on the shows that were being reviewed. (One of my earliest reviews for one of these art journals was suppressed and a kinder critic was asked to do a kinder review). Another, I believe, was the closer relationship that had developed between artists and critics. Often, before reviewing a one-man show, the critic had already visited the artist in his studio, become friendly with him and intoxicated by his personality or the romantic atmosphere surrounding him. Thereafter a dangerous element of hero-worship coloured the critic's attitude to that artist so that he could no longer be an impartial viewer of his work.

But, you are saying (or, maybe, you aren't, but you ought to be) didn't Baudelaire say that the critic should be partial, passionate, and political? He did, and he was right. He would have been appalled at the idea of a critic modifying his opinions about an artist's work because he liked or disliked the artist as a man. The critic's feelings for the artist should have nothing to do with his feelings for his work. Love the artist but damn the work, or damn the artist and love the work, or love them both, or damn them both; the critic must be true to himself. It is a very tall order but according to Michael Fried, one of the most influential American critics, there can be no alternative. In the course of an article attacking the American-based British critic, Lawrence Alloway, he wrote:

206

. . . the true critic has no alternative but to try to determine what is genuine and what is spurious in the art of our time: he has got to make value-judgements, and to defend his choices in the most lucid, intellectually rigorous and visually sensitive manner possible. Any other course of action, call it what one will, reeks of bad faith and deserves to be condemned for the evasion that it is*.

But not all critics would agree that it is the critic's duty to stick his neck out so dangerously as that. Fried's fellow American critic, Kurt von Meier, tells us (in an article attacking Fried for hero-worship!) that, in considering whether an artist's work has art historical significance,

writers on art usually, and quite wisely, apply these tactics: support in print, or at least tacit acceptance of the stature – claims if there seems to be any chance that significance may loom up in time. If not, then there is the recourse of the withheld judgment. No one wants to be out-and-out wrong.†

No one wants to be out-and-out wrong, but, as von Meier adds, of course they still are, unless – and here is the all-important proviso – unless they can

recognise that the present, or imagine that the future, will resolutely refuse to be circumscribed by the standards of the past. The same methodological hang-up – failure to grasp the changes from the past and the unique values of the present – also seriously limits the worth of judgments about intrinsic aesthetic quality.‡

If my limited knowledge of the American language is not at fault, this involved sentence is merely a statement of the obvious fact that you cannot make real value (as distinct from money value) judgments between things of different sorts, that

*In *Art International*, April 1964.
†In *Art International*, 20 October, 1967.
‡*Ibid*.

you cannot judge the qualities of one set of things by the standards of a completely different category of things. For examples (if examples are necessary) you cannot condemn a pig because it cannot fly like a bird, or call a table better than a man because it has four legs.

In the same way, would it not be wrong to say that the marks made by a paint-covered nude woman pressing herself against a canvas are better or worse than a landscape by Van Gogh? Or that human excrement packed in hermetically-sealed tins was better or worse than a Henry Moore sculpture? Of course, you say. But if you say it is wrong because the former item in each example is not, like the latter, a 'work of art', you are mistaken. Here from *Art International* is part of an appreciation of the French artist Yves Klein;

> As spectacle, however, his projects have proven much more rewarding, and, in fact, may be regarded, perhaps, as the true artistic yield of his last period.
>
> The Anthropométries are a good case in point. In 1958, Klein had a model, whose body had been covered with blue paint press herself against a virgin-white canvas in accordance with verbal instructions which he gave her from a distance. During the next two years he carried out increasingly complex experiments based upon the use of the 'living brush'. But the results in every case were inconclusive if not outright bad. Yet Klein's line of reasoning is not without its interest, especially in view of the event to which it led. His monochrome paintings*

*Klein painted his first *monochrome* – a canvas covered with 'one, uniform, scrupulously monochrome colour' – in 1949. In 1956, when he held an exhibition of monochromes of various sizes and colours, the public misinterpreted his intention – 'to free their mind from external contamination, and achieve that stage of contemplation in which colour becomes pure, full sensitivity' – and saw the show as a colourful whole. The following year Klein rammed home the point by exhibiting ten blue paintings that appeared to be exactly the same in every respect. Except one. The prices were all different, a fact that made the viewers examine them minutely and so discover the separate 'essence and atmosphere' of each.

had advanced the idea of depersonalisation in art; the Anthropométries were intended to demonstrate the possibility of still greater detachment: '. . . the purpose . . . was to attain a definite and constant distance between myself and the painting, during the moment of creation.' The event of March 1960, at the Galerie Internationale d'Art Contemporain, Paris, proved the logical culmination of the idea. Before an invited audience, Klein directed the movements of three models to the accompaniment of twenty musicians playing the [Klein's] earlier monotone symphony, a single sound sustained for approximately twenty minutes, preceded and followed by silence. Rejecting the idea that someday he would smear paint over his own body and thus qualify as an ultra-action painter, he made clear his intentions: 'I would rather put on my tuxedo and wear white gloves. I would not even think of dirtying my hands with paint. Detached and distant, the work of art must complete itself before my eyes under my command, thus as soon as the work is realised, I stand there – present at the ceremony, spotless, calm, relaxed, worthy of it, and ready to receive it as it is born into the tangible world.' Here, certainly, is a new variety of aestheticism – shades of Whistler in the guise of a contemporary happening!*

And now, here is the critic Aldo Pellegrini writing about Klein's most faithful pupil, Piero Manzoni (who died in 1963 at thirty):

In an exhibition in 1960 he showed 150 eggs marked with his fingerprint, which were eaten by the public, by which the work of art was considered 'incorporated' directly into the spectator. Then he planned an exhibition of living creatures that would acquire the status of works of art by being signed by him. Evidently this demonstration had its roots in Duchamp's ready-mades, which expressed the idea that mere selection by the artist was enough for any kind of object to become a work

*Sidney Simon, "Yves Klein" Art International, 20 October, 1967.

of art. Manzoni's most aggressive anti-artistic attitude was
contained in his famous series *Merde of the Artist,* which
consisted of fecal matter hermetically packed and labelled with
the weight on the package . . . Manzoni thus reflects the
extreme stand in the negation of all utility of art and in
accentuating his essential and deepest 'invisibility'*

Presumably you are now ready to admit, with me, that the
painting made with the 'living brush' and the *Merde of the
Artist* are works of art (don't let that word 'anti-artistic' worry
you – 'anti-art' is not 'non-art', it's just another sort of art). And
presumably you still think it would be wrong to judge them by
the same standards as those you might apply to the Van Gogh
landscape and the Henry Moore bronze. So, as Mr Meier
implies, we need some new standards by which to judge the
'intrinsic aesthetic quality' of the art of the present. But where
are we to find these new standards, since the whole idea of
standards, along with everything to do with art as we used to
know it, has been rejected by the 'new artists'? Not, it seems,
in the writings of the 'new critics', one of the brightest of
whom, when tackled upon the subject by a reader of *Studio
International,* surprisingly suggested that the enquiry be
referred to that old fuddy-duddy, Lord (formerly Sir Kenneth)
Clark.

The reader (a Mrs Richardson) had written to the magazine
asking artist-critic, Robert Hughes to explain the meaning of
this sentence that had appeared in one of his reviews:

> The "objecthood" of the canvas, thanks largely to the massive
> dominance of Stella and his critics on the international scene,
> has by now become such an article of faith that it obscures other
> issues, such as the need to re-complicate the picture surface once

*Aldo Pellegrini, *New Tendencies in Art.*

the initial statement of its programmatic purity has become a general reflex.

A reasonable request, you might think. But Mr Hughes replied haughtily from the critical tower of Babel:

> . . . in *Studio International* I am writing for a specialist public, not a general one. This is a trade magazine. Ideas like 'objecthood' of the canvas – the fact that it exists as a thick flat thing, and not simply as a thing on painted card – have been the currency of art discussions for nearly a decade . . . If Mrs Richardson wants 'criticism' as I think she means the word – the writer proclaiming whether he likes the painting or not and tickling the reader to make an act of faith in his sensibility – let her address herself to the works of Nigel Gosling or Sir Kenneth Clark which she might enjoy. I don't believe in taste, in that sense. There have never been any standards by which art could be arraigned in the dock.

Indeed, it is only by convincing ourselves that standards and value-judgments are things of the past that we can accept the art-farce of the present. But we do not have to accept it. In 1970, European Conservation Year, the great brains who govern us, at last got the message that ecologists have been preaching for decades, namely, that the too ready acceptance of every bit of 'scientific progress' must lead to disaster for the human race. All scientific possibilities do not necessarily have to be realised just because they are there. With sufficient determination Man could, says ecologist Nicholas Guppy, *'still choose – among many alternatives – a future that will leave us human (if we find out what that means in time).'**

There is obviously a parallel to be drawn from this that can be related to art. It might be argued that art has been perverted in the same way that science has been perverted. That just as

*Sunday Times, 4 January, 1970

211

lack of control over scientific developments in the past is now threatening Man with a deterioration in his physical state, so, too, will lack of control in the arts bring about a deterioration in the state of his spirit. But before anyone shouts 'Fascism, Totalitarianism', let me say that the sort of control I have in mind – the only sort that can be applied to art without killing art – is self-control, the self-control of artists. If you do not like the word self-control, substitute 'sincerity'. Art has become debased through a lack of sincerity, and not only among artists, or even critics, but also among the public. The three groups have been practising a vast mutual confidence trick ever since the heresy that art is for everyone (with its inevitable levelling down of standards) first became popular.

The critic who is brave enough and strong enough to stand outside this vicious triangle has a vital part to play in a tremendously important task during the next few years. It is simply, the saving of living art, a task no less important and no less formidable than that of saving the elements upon which we depend for our physical survival. He (or she) must expose insincerity wherever he finds it (yes, even in these pages!). There is enough of it to keep us all going full time. For all our boasting of our new found permissiveness, freedom, lack of inhibitions, frankness – call it what we will – we are less honest than our parents or grandparents were. And our artists are no exceptions. Grandfather, still painting landscapes in a style that, without his knowledge, had died years before, was more honest than the student just out of the Royal College whose first thought is, 'What crazy thing can I do that will make people notice me?'

It is not without significance that the principal publication devoted to contemporary art in Britain, *Studio International*, has in recent years given more and more of its space to artists writing about art and less and less to art critics. The critics themselves may well be largely to blame, but to believe that because they are dull they can be dispensed with, is dangerous. Critics who are occasionally, or even frequently, prejudiced in favour of a particular artist are far less dangerous than artists-turned-critics who are prejudiced in favour of themselves. The readiness with which today's artists rush into print with 'statements' about their work, their aims, their ideas, their lives, has led to the belief that artists are their own best critics.

Of course, some of them do write well about their own work, but the majority do not. Nevertheless, the articulate ones have succeeded in reversing the old critic-artist relationship, in which the simple artist did not know what he had created until the great critic came along and explained it to him. Thereafter, the artist used the critic's words to explain his work to others, and finally he came to believe they were true. Now, we see the opposite happening. It is the fashion for exhibition catalogues to include notes by the artists about themselves. The critic who begins by welcoming such notes soon becomes dependent upon them. They are usually very plausible. And they are often incomprehensible, which adds to their plausibility and makes it virtually impossible for the critic to dispute them. He can only pretend to understand what the artist is saying, and quote him at length in his review. How else can he react to, for example, this 'artist's statement':

> *Visual Homeostatic Information Mesh* has been structured so that the audience realise the potential and acquire the implications of the conceptual models which have been the determinants for this project, through involving them directly in cognitive processes towards Homeostasis through interactive and essen-

tially self-determined behaviour between themselves and other people using the Mesh as a response system, the area in front (ie The Humps) acting as a control. The project is designed so that a level of partial interaction and as a result partial control can be realised and achieved quickly by an audience, but this can extend to a point of full operation as they acquire the constructs of the control system. The amount of control exercised by a person is directly related to the state of their parameter finding behaviour with the presented context.*

The day when artists declined to speak or write about their work, on the grounds that 'the work speaks for itself', is long gone. Now, artists have turned writers and many of them seem to spend more time writing than in creating art. The Minimalists, in particular, having reduced their art to a minimum, spend most of their time writing. So now we have an extraordinary situation in which art critics are increasingly being forced to relinquish their true function to word-spinning, whizz-kid artists and occupy themselves with criticism, not of the artist's art but his ideas about art and his literary ability in expressing those ideas.

In the April 1969 issue of *Studio International,* critic Barbara Reise named five minimal artists who 'write frequently and well'. Among them was Don Judd, whose criticism, she said 'made significant contributions to the language and approach of art criticism which have only been partially explored'. As if to confirm this laudatory assessment, Mr Judd had contributed a piece of criticism to the same issue of *Studio International.* It included these two contributions to the language of art criticism:

*Stephen Willats, in catalogue of *Kinetics* exhibition, Hayward Gallery, London, 1970.

The last sentence is in the category of 'if the queen had balls, she would be king'.

and:

His pedantic pseudo-philosophical analysis is the equivalent of *Art News* purple prose of the late fifties. That prose was only emotional re-creation and Fried's thinking is just formal analysis and both methods used exclusively are shit.

Significantly, the first quotation is part of an attack upon the American art critic, Clement Greenberg, and the second is part of an attack upon American art critic, Michael Fried. Greenberg and Fried, and another American critic, Sidney Tillim, were also lambasted by another of Miss Reise's five writer-artists, Dan Flavin, in the same issue of *Studio International.* Flavin complains that none of these three 'preposterously-praised, presumptuous, self-appointed, self-indulgent, self-inflicting appraisers and moderators on art is known as an artist first'. In other words, the critic ought to be first of all an artist. Down with critics! Yet elsewhere in his article Flavin rails against critics for writing about an artist's work without first talking to the artist:

It is almost as though they wish to have the man in question a premature corpse in order not to have their idiosyncratic opinionising disturbed and prejudiced by his residual self-determined knowledge which may be but a telephone call away from potential revelation.

Of course, artists are entitled to attack the critics. Most critics *are* idiots. But let us not forget that most people calling themselves artists today are idiots, too. A genuine critic is only a little harder to find than a genuine artist. If only because there are far fewer critics than artists, there are far fewer phoney critics than there are phoney artists. I speak with the unusual (but not all that unusual) authority of one who has been both phoney artist and phoney critic.

12

No Thanks For The Memory

Artists have been misled into thinking that you have to create something in order to contribute to art. I want to create without creating a thing. I want to create without mass or volume . . . Art is only memory anyway.

MIKE HEIZER

If you go around to galleries you wonder 'Is that all there is to art?' I used to feel a kind of lethargy. But then we broke through the floor and found, right underneath, a vast new world – the earth.

DENNIS OPPENHEIM

Impossible for collectors to collect, for museums to show, for dealers to handle, for critics to appraise, the latest art may seem the latest in frivolity, but it must be recognised as the expression of a radical disenchantment with the present role of art in society.

THOMAS M MESSER

Art will disappear as life gains more equilibrium.

PIET MONDRIAN

I would have liked to end this book as I ended *The Art Game* – on an optimistic note. But although it is nine years since I wrote, under the chapter heading, *The Next Revolution,* of the wonderful prospects for art in the promised technological Utopia the whole thing seems now to be even further away than the year 4000 AD – the time forecast by the most pessimistic believers in Utopias. Even before the end of the sixties the new 'art of the technological age' had begun to show signs of the disillusionment that nearly all of us who are not scientists now feel about nearly all the 'miracles' of technology. Artists had gone into the protest business and, whether they knew it or not, what they were protesting against was the *threat* of the promised golden age. However that may be their aim, so far as we the art gamesmen were concerned, was the same as that of the technological utopianists. They wanted to put us out of business, not in 4000 AD but as soon as possible. Under a large variety of labels – Minimalist Art, Concept Art, Anti-Form, Micro-emotive Art, Impossible Art, Possible Art, etc – they endeavoured to create unsaleable art. (They have largely failed so far because they are up against a new breed of museum-wallahs, wheeler-dealers, and collector-investors who accept Kurt Schwitters's definition 'everything the artist spits is art' and Piero Manzoni's modification, by one letter, of that definition.

Ironically, while claiming (as usual) to be art's *avant-garde,* most of these protestants found themselves under the same reactionary banner, 'Balls to technological progress', as the diehard army that still believes painting with brushes on canvas will be with us forever. But whereas the latter shut themselves up in their studios and quietly got on with the job of producing junk for posterity, the former – well, some of them

– started throwing mud, literally. This mud-slinging art – its practitioners call it, grandiloquently, Earth Art – first hit me when the American magazine *Artforum* published a photograph of the interior of the Heiner Friedrich Gallery, Munich, its newly-painted walls completely bare, but its floor carpeted ankle-deep with 'wall to wall dirt', 1600 cubic feet of it!

This recalled for me the occasion, in the late 1950s, when members of the French 'Happenings Movement' had filled a Paris art gallery from floor to ceiling with garbage from the city's refuse carts. But that was a good, though far-fetched, satirical joke if you bear in mind how often art galleries are filled with rubbish erroneously described as art. The Munich event had no such satirical overtones. The word 'dirt' is an American synonym for 'earth'. The photograph was accompanied by a deadly-serious article, *Earth-works and the New Picturesque,* in which the critic and artist, Sidney Tillim, proffered the opinion that Earth Art is a twentieth-century version of the *picturesque,* that theory of landscape which dominated late eighteenth-century and early nineteenth-century English artists:

> As the word itself implies, the picturesque referred to landscape seen in an essentially pictorial way. Landscapes were judged for their pictorial beauties and the same effects in painting were highly praised. In other words it was a way of seeing nature and the setting was very important . . . Minimalist art [the term includes Earth Art] is likewise dependent on setting. Whether of the technological, and hard-edged sort, or the geological and much softer kind, minimalist art is a form of man-made nature or nature made over by man. It does not present objects with art on them but useless artifacts that create a setting rather than a space. The relationship, then, between an observer of minimalist art, or a minimalist object-scape, call it,

219

is analogous to the relationship between the cultivated man of taste and his picturesque view.*

I cannot pretend to understand all of that or to be able to follow its logic (indeed, if I could I would suspect that I was going mad), but to be fair to Mr Tillim I must attempt to précis more of his article, the 'peg' for which was an 'Erthworks' exhibition at the Dwan Gallery, New York. The exhibits were of two kinds, either works actually made from earth ('dirt', soil, sand, or the like) or photographs of 'works' made elsewhere in natural surroundings and impossible of transportation to the gallery. For example, Walter de Maria, the man who did the 'dirt' job in Munich, showed a photograph of a major work – two parallel white chalk lines, a mile long, drawn across the Mojave Desert in California. His friend Michael Heizer was represented by photographs of slit trenches he had dug in remote forests and mud-flats.

Pop artist Claes Oldenburg, famous for his giant coloured-plaster hamburger and baked potato, and for his 'soft' typewriter, water-closet and wash-basin, contributed to the Earthworks show a plastic container filled with 'dirt' said to be seeded with worms, and – wait for it – a film showing the hole he had made when he dug the 'dirt' from a site behind the Metropolitan Museum. Dennis Oppenheim (author of the quotation at the beginning of this chapter) contributed what was, unintentionally no doubt, the show's nearest approach to an orthodox work of art – a model, made from coco-matting, representing a vast wheatfield in which he planned to cut 'rings up to ten miles wide' during the following summer. (Whether he ever carried out this project and what the owner of the wheatfield said I am not, regretfully, able to report). Robert

*Sidney Tillim, 'Earthworks and the New Picturesque', *Artforum*, Dec 1968.

Morris, an assistant professor at Hunter College, New York, and a dancer and choreographer, dumped into the middle of the gallery a compost of dark soil, peat, and pieces of brick and felt, strips or tubes of steel, aluminium, copper, brass, and zinc, and then laced the heap with a messy sauce of thick black industrial grease.

Early in 1969 these American earth artists were invited to contribute to an exhibition of new art sponsored by the European division of Philip Morris, the tobacco company, and presented first at the Kunsthalle in Berne, Switzerland, and later that year at the Institute of Contemporary Arts, London, under the title *When Attitudes Becomes Form.* It was the most outlandish 'art' exhibition ever seen in England up to that time. The initial impact (or perhaps lack of impact) of the show was such that the daily newspaper critics failed completely to find words and phrases adequate to describe it. Terence Mullaly, the conservative critic of the *Daily Telegraph,* who might have been expected to fulminate amusingly about it wrote wearily:

> . . . As the visitor stands on the steps at the entrance to the gallery he notices, piled down their left side, a series of small sacks containing various grains. Before him scattered about the floor are such things as wire-mesh, rough pieces of felt, a pile of earth with wire in it, a long strip consisting of a photograph of the floor on which it lies, a neon tube lighting up strips of torn cloth and so on . . .

Evidently Mr Mullaly had been too bored by it all to bother to read his way through the lavish catalogue of the exhibition, otherwise he would have recognised that the catalogue itself was a work of 'new art' whose pretentious absurdity outclassed that of all the exhibits. It began with a brief message, hilariously inept, from the boss of the sponsoring company:

221

The works assembled for this exhibit have been grouped by many observers of the art scene under the heading 'new art'. We at Philip Morris feel it is appropriate that we participate in bringing these works to the attention of the public, for there is a key element in this 'new art' which has its counterpart in the business world. That element is innovation – without which it would be impossible for progress to be made in any segment of society.

Just as the artist endeavours to improve his interpretation and conceptions through innovation, the commercial entity strives to improve its end product or service through experimentation with new methods and materials. Our constant search for a new and better way in which to perform and produce is akin to the questionings of the artists whose works are represented here . . .

Evidently the big-businessman, like Mr Mullaly, had not read and digested the remaining contents of the catalogue. For only by standing on his head could any industrialist find parallels between his business procedures and the deliberately anarchic procedures of the 'new artists' as related in their own statements and that of Mr Harald Szeemann, director of the Kunsthalle and prime instigator of the exhibition, who wrote of increasing numbers of artists working against all the ideas and principles of the society in which they found themselves!

Obviously the American earth artists could not transport large areas of desert or vast chunks of forest to the 'Attitudes' exhibition, so they sent instead photographs of their earlier 'works', plans and specifications of future ones, and photographs of themselves. Michael Heizer sent a photograph of his 1968 opus, *Dissipate No 2* – five neatly-lined trenches 12 ft long by 12 in wide, varying in depth from 12 in at one end to nothing at the other, cut into the sun-cracked mud of Black Rock Desert, Nevada. With it came another, showing Mr Heizer in the desert, leaning nonchalantly against his Chevrolet truck.

When engaged on more recent 'desert sculptures of negative space', Heizer went to work by plane. He found a patron in Mr Robert Scull, the shrewd art collector-investor whose support of the Abstract Expressionists in the 1950s amd the Pop artists in the 1960s had paid off handsomely. But Mr Scull's patronage of Heizer the Earth artist was completely disinterested for there appeared to be no marketable end-product of his art. Interviewed for *Studio International,* Mr Scull explained his association with Heizer in characteristically forthright style:

> A boy calls me up, for example, and says, 'I must make holes in the earth. I must go to the desert and make sculpture.' At first, I said 'What'll I get out of it?' and then I realised that he's doing just what I'd want to do – scratching his initials in the desert. What better way is there to gain status than through culture? Why does this make people angry? So it's ephemeral art – even *The Last Supper* is already a dream. Why must something last 10,000 years? What makes that better? Collectors think there must be some hidden motive in this attitude. But most of the art I have is worth so much more now than what I paid for it, why not give a little back by commissioning unknown artists? How can you just say starve to death instead, and not support them? The easiest thing of all is collecting, but, I've been out of that for a long time. Now I work directly with the artist.

Walter de Maria's offering for 'Attitudes' was an idea that he had already used in a Chicago exhibition – a one-way telephone placed on the floor in the middle of the exhibition, during the run of which the artist would ring up from his New York studio and speak to any visitor who cared to answer. This idea was sent to Harald Szeeman in Berne with this note:

I am enclosing a complete copy of my S.M.S edition of my work entitled *Chicago Project.* The only change would be that the Project (work) when realised in Switzerland . . . would entail the use of 400 dollars' worth of telephone time. I would keep a record of the cost of each call.

Harold [sic] . . . I feel that this is the best work I can submit to you. I believe it does span the entire range of all five categories:

Works, Processes, concepts, situations, information.

I wish you good luck and success with the show.

I am awaiting your reply . . . in regard to the enclosed . . . and material above.

If you are thinking that 400 dollars seems a lot of money for the pleasure of talking to Mr de Maria rest assured that this is one of his cheaper projects. Far cheaper than, for example, his plan to build two half-mile long concrete walls in the Nevada desert (near his friend Heizer's 'sculpture-garden of negative space') and his *Three Continent Project.* For the latter the requirements were: (i) a mile-long ditch dug in the Sahara Desert (ii) a mile-sided square dug in a US desert (iii) a mile-long 'vertical' line dug in India. 'When all of the lines are photographed from the air,' said de Maria, 'the photos are placed one on top of the other, the image will reveal a cross in a square. Three continents are needed for this image, which can be photographed in one day by a satellite.'

Robert Morris, instead of creating one of his 'compost' heaps for the exhibition sent detailed instructions for a 'bonfire piece' to be made by proxy:

1. Collect as many different kinds of combustible materials as are available in Berne – coal, oil, fireplace logs, grass, peat, coke, twigs, magnesium, etc. Assign a curator to think of more than I have listed.

2. Divide the number of exhibition days, less one, by the number of materials.

3. Begin with one material and place it in the allotted space (inside or outside). At each interval obtained by step 2 add another material. Each material must be placed freely in the space – that is, not in containers. If necessary, protect the floor inside with plastic from the beginning.

4. On the last day of the exhibition remove the entire mass (if set up inside) to a designated safe place outside the museum and ignite.

Of course, *When Attitudes Become Form* was by no means confined to Earth art. Mr Szeeman listed several other categories of the 'new art' which were represented – Anti-Form, Micro-Emotive Art, Possible Art, Impossible Art, Concept Art, Arte Povera. Each name he wrote, described only one aspect of the style – the obvious opposition to form; the high degree of personal and emotional engagement (that puzzles me – I should have thought 'micro-emotive' meant the exact opposite); the pronouncement that certain objects are art, although they have not previously been identified as such; the shift of interest away from the result towards the artistic process; the use of mundane materials; the interaction of work and material; Mother Earth as medium, work-place, the desert as concept.

The acute observer of the twentieth-century art scene will know that, in spite of the omnibus term 'new art', there is nothing about any of this that is fundamentally new. The first abstractions of Kandinsky, in 1910-12, were 'anti-form'. The black-pencilled square on white paper, with which Malevich launched Suprematism in 1913 was 'micro-emotive'. Duchamp's 'readymades' of 1914 were 'possible' art (and the artist who stopped me in London's Oxford Street one day in 1960, drew a chalk circle on the pavement around me, and pronounced me a work of art, was obviously an 'impossible' artist). Picabia's *Ironic Machines* of 1919 were a form of 'concept' art, and Schwitters's *Merzbau* of the 1920s was 'poor man's' art. The various forms of Earth Art, which might at first appear to be genuinely 'new', nearly all have precedents in such things as the sand drawings of New Hebridean natives and sand paintings of the Navajo Indians, the white horses and giants carved in our English chalk hills and the barrows and stone circles built by our remote ancestors, or just in the mud-pies we made as children.

Looking back at earlier centuries we can perceive a degree of logic in the way a new movement came to be born, to grow and, sooner or later, to be killed off by a newer movement that reacted against its ideas. This process was not brought about by a group of artists arbitrarily deciding that they must do something new. It was dictated to them by life. Art that does not change with the life of the time in which it exists is not art. In retrospect it is easy to see how the great movements in art belonged to the times in which they were born, but at those times it was usually only the handful of artists immediately concerned who understood what they were about. The rest of the world, if it took any interest at all in the event, saw the new movement as a violation of art as they had always (they thought) known it.

In our day the gap between the emergence of a new movement in art and its recognition or acceptance by the art-conscious public has been diminishing by geometrical progression. It is now only a matter of a few years before a new movement becomes an old movement, takes its place in the museums and is endowed with that quality of 'pastness' that, as critic Lionel Trilling has remarked, 'gives it an extra aesthetic authority which is incorporated into its aesthetic power'. It is already a long time since Abstract Expressionism became museum stuff and its leading exponents, Jackson Pollock*, Franz Kline, Willem de Kooning and Co are now hallowed old masters. As early as April 1970 the King of Pop art, Richard Hamilton, was being canonised at the Tate Gallery, where the movement he pioneered had already been allotted a place in the official history of British art. And in 1974 the Tate has contrived to prove that the New Art, under whatever name it comes, is not *(pace* Mr Messer) 'impossible for museums to show'. Throughout that year two of its rooms were devoted to the systematic exhibition of 'important acquisitions of works of art' representing various forms of the New Art, 'from Minimal to Conceptual'. The fact that you, a normally intelligent man or woman, may still think that the examples of the New Art that I have described are not art does not matter a damn. For, remember Harold Rosenberg – 'Art comes to be a balance among the things it is asserted to be by the self-elected individuals who create it and devote themselves to it.'

In recent times, when extraordinary modes of artistic expression have proliferated like weeds, and become entangled with each other, we have been confronted every few months with a 'new' *avant garde*. Like the Dadaists, fifty years earlier, the originators of most of these movements believe, with as much sincerity as they are capable of, that our precious Art-with-a-capital-A is dead. But, again like the Dadaists, the things they create (or don't create) in order to prove that Art is no

*In 1973 the Australian National Gallery paid £800,000 for Pollock's painting, *The Blue Poles.*

227

more, are themselves assimilated by the brainwashed art-pundits and avaricious art-mongers as works of Art. So the would-be art revolutionist must go beyond art to politics and philosophy if he is ever to see the old capital-A-art buried for ever and a new concept of art take its place.

In the past individual artists (unlike writers) have had little effect politically upon society. Even Goya, Gillray, Courbet, Grosz, Heartfield were no more than small thorns in the sides of their enemies. Nor have those art movements, such as Futurism, Dadaism and Surrealism, which embraced political aims, been any more effective. One reason for this is that, until now, the public has regarded the artist as an outsider, a fellow who lives in the clouds, a child in worldly affairs, a radical, perhaps, but not a dangerous radical. Today the image of the artist is changing. And so is the attitude of the public towards him. The genuine artist of today (that rare being) is often an aggressive, articulate, political animal, who uses his art for political ends of the most far-reaching kind. He does not create propagandist art to further the narrow aims of a particular party. If he thinks about political parties at all he sees them as excrescences that must be swept away, along with all those other manifestations of our moribund civilisation, manifestations that include practically everything that I, and probably you, were brought up to believe was art. Temporarily he is a nihilist. He believes that all the old values must be swept away before the new ones can be created. He believes that art must be reborn one day but his immediate concern is to hasten the death of Art. Individually he may be seduced by the fruits of success in the world he has sworn to destroy, but his place will immediately be taken by two new crusaders and the fight will go on. Already it has been more successful than most of us realise.

Whether we, the art gamesmen, like it or not, the nails are relentlessly being punched into the coffin of our reactionary trade. The frenzied and much-vaunted new explosion of interest in art that we have seen in recent years has nothing to do with art and everything to do with money. We have never had it so good, and art itself has never had it so bad. And when you come to think seriously about it this unity of opposites must be as old as the art market. A successful art market must be inimical to true art, and if one thrives the other must sicken – and maybe die. Art is certainly sickening and the market is certainly thriving, and we are further away than ever from Mondrian's (and others') dream of a life so serene that art will be unnecessary. So the art market that is thriving largely upon dead old art and stillborn new art, must die in order that true art may live. True art? What the hell is true art? you may ask, and I have to confess that it is easier to say what it is not than what it is. It is not a hedge against inflation for a fat financier or a meal-ticket for a hungry artist. It is not a clever piece of work by a deserving craftsman or a prophylactic for a millionaire with an inferiority complex. It is not a 'primitive' painting by a sophisticated grandmother or a wise investment for a wealthy widow. It is not a Renaissance portrait by a living Italian 'genius' or a solid gold cast of a trite figure of clay. It is not a signed reproduction of a painting by a fashionable hack or yet one more original lithograph by the once original Old Moore. It is not everything that an artist does nor anything that a non-artist does. It is an artist's *cri de coeur* (and not just any old artist's *coeur*). It is price-less and priceless, value-less and invaluable. It comes in an infinite number of guises. It could even be a slit-trench in a desert – until a speculator sponsors it; or a dung heap in a dance-hall – until an art dealer deals in it;

229

or a strip-light in a studio – until Sothebys sell it.*

Enough of rhetoric. It does not take a very brilliant mind to see that something is very rotten in the state of art, and that that rottenness is only a part of the general decay of Western civilisation. No wonder, then, that most artists, art historians or critics who are concerned about the future of art end by finding comfort only in dreams of distant Utopias such as Constant Nieuwenhuy's 'New Babylon' in which,

> since all the work will be done by machines . . . the energies now devoted to work will be spent on the development of man's creative capacities in the world-wide city which will be a sort of enormous playground.‡

Yes. But what about now? At the present time when there is a world-wide 'energy crisis', when Britain is faced with economic problems it cannot solve, the New Babylon seems much further away even than 4000 AD. Clearly Nieuwenhuys's call to the creative man of ten years ago to 'prepare a new exciting reality based on the actual possibilities of technical production, instead of depicting and expressing the unsatisfying and stagnant reality that is about to be liquidated', fell almost entirely upon deaf ears. The unsatisfying and stagnant reality is still with us and the creative man's responses to it, or escapes from it, become more and more puerile. Why?

Of the great avalanche of art books published during the past ten years I can recall only one that asks that question and seeks to answer it in a fashion that, as Sickert put it sixty years ago, 'takes no highfalutin ground for art'. In spite of its gimmicky title, *Fads, Fakes and Forgeries*‡ is a serious book. As its subtitle

---

*An arrangement of three red and three yellow neon tubes, by Dan Flavin was sold for £4,000 at Sotheby's on 5 July, 1973. Another, of five tubes, made £4,800 in 1974.
†*ICA Bulletin,* No 140, October 1964
‡Macdonald, 1970

– *The Crisis in the Art Schools and the Crisis in Art* – suggests, its author, Sjoerd Hannema, an artist and Lecturer in the History of Art at Manchester Polytechnic, believes that the rot begins in the art schools. In spite of the great shake-up envisaged in the early 1960s, when our art colleges were given university status, art education is still largely devoted to what William Morris called 'art for the swinish luxury of the rich'. It still perpetuates the myth that artists are men apart (especially apart from craftsmen). By clinging to 'fine art' as its central discipline and by offering a preponderance of courses in painting and sculpture, as against courses in design and various crafts, it encourages a majority of students to squander what modest talents they have in dreams of becoming famous – and rich – artists. It encourages them to opt for the art rat-race in which only one in thousands of them can possibly win a prize, i e a place in the 'stable' of a successful art-dealer. It leaves them disgruntled and totally unprepared for any role in life except that of 'failed artist'. (And, sadly, it is from the ranks of these disgruntled failed artists that most of our art-teachers are drawn). It has, says Hannema, made the education of artists 'as speculative as the art trade itself with Mayfair, hub of the world fashion, setting the pace in both'. It would be comforting of course, to think that we had only to reorganise our art educational system to save art from the fate worse than death that seems already to have befallen it. But it would be foolish, and no one realises it better than Hannema. The reform of art education would, he says,

> only achieve its real purpose if it served as a forerunner of
> fundamental social reform. The artist of the future would then
> find his true calling in an egalitarian society in which all people
> harmoniously participated in a creative, artistic life. In such a

socialist society art would become the sum total of collective, creative action.

So we are back to utopias again. Unlike most artist's Utopias, Hannema's would be based on Christian principles. But, like theirs, his dream is also founded on the assumption that the world is heading for an 'era of leisure' brought about by the advance of technology. Personally, I do not think we are ever going to make it.

If Winter Comes

In this place in *The Art Game* I asked the question 'Will the boom last?' and, in spite of a pessimistic nature, gave a largely reassuring answer. In the event, however, even more optimism would not have been misplaced. The boom has continued to boom almost continuously since 1965 and has attained a magnitude that no one, not even the chairman of Sotheby's (who chided me some years ago for daring to suggest the possibility that art prices might some day 'level-off') can have foreseen. And yet, while each day brings new record prices that bear witness to ever increasing faith in the superiority of art as investment, a make-hay-while-the-sun-shines attitude pervades the art trade. From the stalls of Portobello Road to the salons of Sotheby-Parke Bernet the art gamesmen behave as if every possible paltry pound must be raked in and stored up for a long hard winter.

A decade has passed since I first noted that 'every cry of woe from the Stock Exchange is countered by a whoop of joy at some new record price paid in the Bond Street and King Street market places'. In 1974 this irrational sequence of cause and effect was being repeated, but at a higher level. The cries were cries of desperation, the whoops were much wilder than before. The 'City' pages of the newspapers repeatedly advised their readers to get into art and antiques as the best hedges against raging inflation. The response, headed by bankers and investment brokers, was so enormous that I felt sure the *Wall Street Journal* (and the *Financial Times*) were about to come up with that art-exchange page, based on Dow-Jones averaging techniques, that we read about in Chapter 2. But, I wondered, if art is to be treated as just another commodity for the world's stock exchanges to gamble with, will it not be just as susceptible to the market's vagaries as any other commodity? Since the roaring art prices of 1973/4 were largely the result of panic selling by refugees from stocks and shares, could not panic selling by such people equally easily send the prices down again?

I am only asking the question, I don't know the answer. Nor, I am interested to learn, does art-economics expert Gerald Reitlinger, who says:

> We have yet to learn the meaning of an economic depression to an art market dominated by high-pressure sales promotion.*

There are no precedents for the present art boom nor any for the way in which it may end, but Reitlinger, looking back to the great depression of the Thirties notes a number of phenomena that may still have relevance in our time. For example, he points out that the extreme vulnerability of the market for eighteenth-century English portraits, a market in which Duveen was king, was not due to over-promotion alone but also to the fact that such portraits belonged to a taste that was

*The Times, March 21, 1974

234

proving too conservative, a taste for things that had stayed dear simply because rich men had been running them up for nearly a century.

It might be thought that today the Impressionists occupy the place that in the Twenties belonged to Gainsborough, Romney, Reynolds and company and that on the assumption that 'the higher they fly the harder they fall', they will make the loudest thud if and when things go wrong. But, as Reitlinger reminds us, today differs enormously from the Thirties when 'the depression struck a market that was selective to the point of artistic snobbery'. Now, the market embraces anything and everything and caters for every taste and no taste. Now Impressionists and Post-Impressionists, Fauves and Expressionists, Abstractionists and Surrealists, Pop and Op and Porn, Erotica, Exotica and Neurotica, Victorians and Edwardians, indoor and outdoor Sporting Artists, and a dozen other categories, have all been over-promoted and over-priced. And along with them go the loads of rubbish that opportunist auctioneers knock down to the collecting-crazy public – old beer, boots, bottles, buttons, Christmas-crackers, cigarette-cards, dolls, doylies, fruit-box labels, lead soldiers, matchboxes, menu-cards, photographs, postcards, swizzle sticks, tin toys, tobacco tins, underwear, walking-sticks, winkle-picks, xylographs, yoghourt tubs, zincos – you name it, someone somewhere collects it, probably as a hedge against inflation!

For the true art collector, if he exists anywhere anymore, there is consolation in the knowledge that whatever a slump could do to the money value of his treasures it cannot alter their aesthetic value. For the rest of you there is the hopeless hope that only the rubbish will become worthless and your genuine works of art will keep their prices. For the real art gamesman, however, there is no apparent depression about the prospect of a depression, because the evidence of the present is that his lot gets better as the world's economic mess gets worse.

236

INDEX

ABBOTT & HOLDER, 56, 57, 58
Abbott, John White, 56
Abrams, Harry, 61
Adams, Robert, 51
Adeney, Bernard, 51
Agar, Eileen, 51
Agnew, Sir Geoffrey, 40, 176, 183
Agnew's, 37, 40, 84-86, 101, 155, 178-179, 180, 184, 185, 189, 191, 199
Alloway, Lawrence, 206
Anderson, Stanley, 54
Andrea del Sarto, 92
Angerstein, John Julius, 24
Angrand, Charles, 78
Armstrong, John, 51
Artemis, 12
Artforum, 219
Art International, 207, 208
Art News, 215
Athena Prints, 114
Atkinson, Laurence, 51
Austin, Robert, 54
Austria, Archduke Leopold of, 23
Aylesford, Earl of, (Heneage Finch), 56
Aylesford, Countess of, 56

BACHE, JULES, 25, 26
Bacon, Francis, 62, 195
Badmin, S R, 54
Bainbridge, John, 28
Balanci, 205
Baldung Grien, Hans, 152
Ball, Ian, 97
Bampfylde, C W, 56
Banting, John, 51
Banque Lambert, 12
Barber, Noel, 16
Baring, Maj Edward, 40
Bartolommeo, Fra, 178
Bateman, H M, 57
Baudelaire, Charles, 206
Bauer, Marius A J, 54
Baur, John I H, 45
Bawden, Edward, 51, 54
Baynes, Keith, 51
Beauclerk, Lady Diana, 56
Beaumont, Sir George, 56
Behrman, S N, 25, 102, 200
Bell, Clive, 203
Bell, Graham, 51
Bell, R Anning, 58
Bellingham-Smith, H, 58
Bellini, Giovanni, 103
Berenson, Bernard, 89, 102, 103, 104
Berger, John, 92, 97
Bevan, Robert, 50
Bigge, John Selby, 51
Blampied, Edmund, 54
Bland, E Beatrice, 51
Bliss, Douglas, 54
Bomberg, David, 81
Bone, Sir Muirhead, 54
Bonham's, 151, 153-156
Botticelli, 37
Boxall, Sir William, 57
Bracquemond, Felix, 54
Bradley, Helen, 114
Brammer, Leonard G, 54
Brancusi, Constantin, 205
Brangwyn, Sir Frank, 28, 54
Brausen, Erica, 196
Bree, Rev William, 56
Brill, Reginald, 54
Brilliant, Fredda, 145
Briscoe, Arthur, 54
British Museum, 90-91, 107, 143, 159, 191
Brock, C E, 57
Brock, H M, 57
Brockhurst, Gerald, 54
Brown, Ford Madox, 140
Browne, Hablot K, 57
Brunery, François, 49
Buckland-Wright, John, 54
Buckley, C F, 57
Butcher, Enid, 54

CAIN, CHARLES W, 54
Camden Town Group, 51
Cameron, Sir D Y, 54
Canaday, John, 71, 84
Canetti, Elias, 160
Carleton, Sir Dudley, 106, 153
Carr, Thomas, 52
Carter, John, 69
Cattermole, Charles, 57
Cattermole, George, 57
Cattrell, Mrs V G, 152
Cézanne, Paul, 35, 100, 162
Chadwick, Tom, 55
Chagall, Marc, 96-7
Chance, I O 'Peter', 176-8
Chardin, J B S, 140
Charles I, 22, 153
Charles II, 22-3
Charles, James, 58
Cheston, C S, 55
Christie's, 36, 40, 42, 44, 45, 49, 69, 71, 75, 76, 77, 78, 79, 84, 87, 101, 103, 115, 117, 118, 123, 133, 137, 145, 146, 160, 161, 162, 170, 175-8, 183, 185, 188, 189
Clark, Lord (Kenneth), 90, 139, 210-211
Claude Lorrain, 140
Clausen, Sir George, 58
Cleveland Museum of Art, 104, 106
Clough, Prunella, 52
Clutton-Brock, Alan, 52
Coe's (Debenham Coe), 156
Collins, Cecil, 52
Colnaghi's, 178, 180
Colquhoun, Robert, 55
Connard, Philip, 52
Constable, John, 108, 113, 140
Cook Collection, 175
Cook, Sir Francis, 178
Cook, Lady, 178
Corot, J B C, 90, 108, 121, 122
Cotman, John Sell, 122
Courbet, Gustave, 228
Cowdray, Lord, 153
Coxon, Raymond, 52
Cozens, John Robert, 191
Cranach, Lucas, 152
Croegart, Georges, 49
Croft, Ernest, 57
Cromwell, Oliver, 22
Crosland, Anthony, 125
Crotch, Dr William, 56
Cundall, Charles, 140
Cuyp, Aelbert, 45

DACRE, WINIFRED, 52
Daily Mail, The, 125, 130, 137, 141
Daily Telegraph, The, 12, 42, 43, 47, 114, 221
Daily Telegraph Magazine, 96-7
Dali, Salvador, 95
Dalou, Jules, 146-7
Dart, R Poussette, 52
Daumier, Honoré, 71, 109, 110
David, Hermine, 55
Dawson, Montague, 114
Day, James Wentworth, 140-141
De Blaas, Eugene, 49
De Chirico, Giorgio, 81
De Dreux, Alfred, 157-8
De Hory, Elmyr, 98-100
De Kooning, Willem, 60, 61, 65, 66, 227
De Largillière, Nicolas, 39
De Maria, Walter, 220, 223-4
Derain, André, 98, 100
De Vos, Cornelis, 154
De Wint, Peter, 122
Dicksie, Sir Frank, 57
Dismorr, Jessica, 52
Dobson, Frank, 52
Dodd, Francis, 55
Dodgson, John, 52
Dommersen, P C and W, 49
Dotremont, Philippe, 59, 66
Drummond, Malcolm, 52
Drury, Paul, 55
Duccio, 125
Duchamp, Marcel, 209, 225
Dufy, Raoul, 98, 100

239

240